ACCUPLACER TEST SUCCESS

Accuplacer Practice Tests

TABLE OF CONTENTS

Accuplacer Test Information

The Accuplacer Test is a placement test that your college will administer in order to assess your skills in English and math. The Accuplacer is a computer-adaptive test. This means that you will take the test on a computer and that your response to previous questions will determine the difficulty level of subsequent questions. In other words, if you continue to answer all of the questions correctly, the questions generally should get more difficult as the test progresses.

Test questions on the Accuplacer Test are multiple-choice. When you take the actual test on the computer, the question will appear on one side of the screen and the answer choices will appear on the other side.

Since the Accuplacer is a secure test, the items in this book are not actual test questions. However, this practice material is designed to simulate the difficulty level that the majority of students will face on the actual test.

Note: Accuplacer is a registered trademark of the College Entrance Examination Board, which is not affiliated with nor endorses this publication.

ACCUPLACER PRACTICE TEST 1

1. *Select the best substitute for the underlined parts of the following ten sentences. The first answer [choice A] is identical to the original sentence. If you think the original sentence is best, then choose A as your answer.*

   Although she was only sixteen years old, <u>the university accepted her application because of her outstanding grades</u>.
   - A.   the university accepted her application because of her outstanding grades.
   - B.   her application was accepted by the university because of her outstanding grades.
   - C.   her outstanding grades resulted in her application being accepted by the university.
   - D.   she was accepted to study at the university after applying because of her outstanding grades.

2. Never in my life <u>have I seen such a beautiful sight.</u>
   - A.   have I seen such a beautiful sight.
   - B.   I have seen such a beautiful sight
   - C.   such a beautiful sight I have seen.
   - D.   such a beautiful sight I saw.

3. After the loss of a loved one, the bereaved can experience <u>shock, numbness, and they also get depressed.</u>
   - A.   shock, numbness, and they also get depressed.
   - B.   shock, numbness, and depression.
   - C.   shock, numbness, and get depressed.
   - D.   shock, numbness, and depressed.

4. I was going to studying this <u>evening, however the noise next door</u> made it impossible.
   - A.   evening, however the noise next door
   - B.   evening: however the noise next door
   - C.   evening, however, the noise next door
   - D.   evening. However, the noise next door

5. She was hoping to buy <u>a new car which would be spacious enough to transport</u> her equipment.
   - A.   a new car which would be spacious enough to transport
   - B.   a new car, which would be spacious enough to transport
   - C.   a new car – which would be spacious enough to transport
   - D.   a new car, that would be spacious enough to transport

6. Near a small <u>river, at the bottom of the canyon we discovered a cave.</u>
   - A.   river, at the bottom of the canyon we discovered a cave.
   - B.   river at the bottom of the canyon we discovered a cave.
   - C.   river at the bottom of the canyon, we discovered a cave.
   - D.   river, at the bottom of the canyon, we discovered, a cave.

7. <u>Who did the interview panel select</u> for the job?
   - A.   Who did the interview panel select
   - B.   Whom did the interview panel select
   - C.   Who the interview panel selected
   - D.   Whom the interview panel selected

1

8. They played <u>the song "Always and Forever"</u> at their wedding reception.
    A. the song "Always and Forever"
    B. the song, "Always and Forever,"
    C. the song "Always and Forever,"
    D. the song "Always and Forever",

9. He lost his <u>scholarship, as a consequence of his poor grades.</u>
    A. scholarship, as a consequence of his poor grades.
    B. scholarship as a consequence of his poor grades.
    C. scholarship, as a consequence his poor grades.
    D. scholarship, as a consequence of, his poor grades.

10. <u>If I was a millionaire, I would give</u> money to charity.
    A. If I was a millionaire, I would give
    B. If I was a millionaire, I will give
    C. If I were a millionaire, I would give
    D. If I were a millionaire, I will give

11. *Rewrite the following ten sentences mentally in your own head. Follow the directions given for the formation of the new sentence. Remember that your new sentence should be grammatically correct and convey the same meaning as the original sentence.*

She worked all night, but she still did not finish the project. Rewrite, beginning with: <u>Even though</u>

The next words will be:
    A. she working all night
    B. she worked all night
    C. working all night
    D. worked all night

12. *While snow showers are common in the north during the winter, precipitation is unlikely tomorrow.* Rewrite, beginning with: <u>Despite</u>

The next words will be:
    A. snow showers are common
    B. of snow showers being common
    C. snow showers being common
    D. snow showers as common

13. *Warm all year round, Florida has many out-of-state visitors during December and January.* Rewrite, beginning with: <u>Because</u>

The next words will be:
    A. warm all year round,
    B. of warm all year round,
    C. of all-year-round warm,
    D. it is warm all year round,

14. *Tom is highly intelligent, and so is his younger brother.* Rewrite, beginning with: <u>Just as</u>

    Your new sentence will include:
    - A. so too is his younger brother
    - B. as well as his younger brother
    - C. in the same way, his younger brother
    - D. his younger brother, similarly

15. *Mary arrived at the party. Then I decided to go home.* Rewrite, beginning with: <u>After</u>

    The next words will be:
    - A. Mary arriving at the party
    - B. Mary had arrived at the party
    - C. arriving at the party
    - D. arrived at the party

16. *You will succeed at college if you work hard.* Rewrite, beginning with: <u>Provided</u>

    The next words will be:
    - A. hard work
    - B. work hard
    - C. you work hard
    - D. that your work hard

17. *She is a good teacher because she is kind and patient.* Rewrite, beginning with: <u>Kind and patient</u>

    Your new sentence will include:
    - A. of a good teacher
    - B. is a good teacher
    - C. make a good teacher
    - D. which a good teacher

18. *Apart from being rude, she is also stingy.* Rewrite, beginning with: <u>Besides</u>

    The next words will be:
    - A. being rude
    - B. of being rude
    - C. of rudeness
    - D. she is rude

19. *The teacher became upset because the student was insolent.* Rewrite, beginning with: <u>Because of</u>

    The next words will be:
    - A. being upset
    - B. the teacher was upset
    - C. the student was insolent
    - D. the student's insolence

3

20. *More and more teenagers are developing type II diabetes.* Rewrite, beginning with: Increasing

   The next words will be:
   A. teenagers
   B. teenage diabetes
   C. numbers of teenagers
   D. amount of teenagers

21. *For the following ten questions, read the passage and then select the correct answer to the question. You may need to answer based on explicit information from the passage, as well as ideas that are suggested or implied in the passage.*

   Research shows that the recent rise in teenage smoking has primarily taken place in youth from more affluent families, whose parents are both working. Therefore, these teenagers are not from disadvantaged homes, as most people seem to believe. The facts demonstrate quite the opposite because the most striking and precipitous rise in smoking has been for teenagers from the most financially advantageous backgrounds.

   What is the primary purpose of this passage?
   A. to provide information on a recent trend
   B. to emphasize the dangers of smoking
   C. to dispel a common misconception
   D. to highlight the difference between two types of teenagers

22. Gene splicing, the process whereby a small part of the DNA of one organism is removed and inserted into the DNA chain of another organism, has produced results like the super tomato. In order to create the super tomato, the gene resistant to cold temperatures on the DNA chain of a particular type of cold-water fish was isolated, removed, and inserted into an ordinary tomato plant. This resulted in a new type of tomato plant that can thrive in cold weather conditions.

   From this passage, it seems safe to conclude that
   A. the super tomato was the first case of gene splicing.
   B. the super tomato is only one example of gene splicing.
   C. DNA from tomatoes has also been inserted into certain types of fish.
   D. many people object to gene splicing.

23. In 1804, Meriwether Lewis and William Clark began an expedition across the western United States, then known as the Louisiana Territory. The two men had met years earlier and established a long-lasting friendship. When Lewis was later a young captain in the army, he received a letter from President Thomas Jefferson offering him funding to explore the western country. With Jefferson's permission, Lewis offered a partnership in the expedition to his friend Clark. When their journey had safely concluded 8,000 miles later, President Jefferson purchased the Louisiana Territory for fifteen million dollars.

   The purpose of the passage is
   A. to give the background to Lewis and Clark's westward expedition.
   B. to defend the purchase of the Louisiana Territory.
   C. to state a crucial decision made by Thomas Jefferson.
   D. to compare the skills of Lewis and Clark.

24. The Watergate burglary had many aspects, but at its center was President Richard Nixon. Throughout the investigation of the burglary, government officials denied involvement in the crime. An extensive cover-up operation followed in an attempt to conceal those who were involved in planning the break-in. Yet, this subterfuge failed when the FBI investigated the one hundred dollars bills that were found in the pockets of the burglars. After making inquiries, the FBI discovered that this money originated from the Committee for the Re-election of the President, thereby confirming governmental involvement. In the end, individuals who had entered the highest branches of the American government to serve and protect the people went to prison instead.

What is main reason why the cover-up of the Watergate break-in failed?
  A.   because the Committee for the Re-election of the President denied involvement
  B.   because of the subterfuge of the FBI
  C.   because the burglars' money was traced back to a governmental organization
  D.   because its ringleaders went to prison

25. Organic farming has become one of the fastest growing trends in agriculture recently. Over the past ten years, sales of organic products in the United States have increased a staggering 20 percent, with retail sales per year of more than 9 billion dollars. American farmers have realized that organic farming is an incredibly cost-effective method because it can potentially be used to control costs, as well as to appeal to higher-priced markets. Apart from these monetary benefits, organic farming also results in positive ecological outcomes for the environment because the use of chemicals and synthetic materials is prohibited.

The main idea of the paragraph is that organic farming
  A.   is a very profitable sector of the agricultural industry.
  B.   was less popular ten years ago.
  C.   prohibits chemical and synthetic materials.
  D.   has grown in popularity recently because it is cost-effective and environmentally-friendly.

26. Cancer occurs when cells in the body begin to divide abnormally and form more cells without control or order. There are some factors which are known to increase the risk of cancer. Smoking is the largest single cause of death from cancer in the United States. In addition, poor food choices increase cancer risk. Indeed, research shows that there is a definite link between the consumption of high-fat food and cancer.

From this passage, we can infer that
  A.   a low-fat diet can reduce the risk of cancer.
  B.   smoking usually causes cells to divide abnormally.
  C.   the consumption of high-fat food has increased in recent years.
  D.   most cancer sufferers have made poor food choices.

27. The theory of multiple intelligence (MI) is rapidly replacing the intelligence quotient, or IQ. The IQ, long considered the only valid way of measuring intelligence, has come under criticism because it inheres in many cultural biases. For this reason, there has been a movement away from the IQ test, which is now seen as an indication of a person's academic ability. On the other hand, multiple intelligence measures practical skills such as spatial, visual, and musical ability.

   The main idea of the passage is that
   A. there are cultural biases in the IQ test.
   B. the IQ does not take visual or spatial ability into account.
   C. the theory of multiple intelligence is superior to the concept of IQ.
   D. multiple intelligence is a measure of an individual's practical abilities.

28. Around the world today, more than a billion people still do not have fresh, clean drinking water available on a daily basis. Hundreds of thousands of people in developing countries die needlessly every year because of the consumption of unclean, disease-ridden water. Simply stated, fresh water saves lives. However, what has been understood only recently is that the provision for fresh water around the globe also protects the environment because it means that those who manage water supplies must evaluate in more detail why and how developed countries consume and pollute their available water. Without this evaluation, an ever-increasing number of individuals will continue to die from water-related diseases.

   We can conclude from the information in this passage that
   A. water-related disease will decline in the future.
   B. water-related deaths could be avoided.
   C. children are the most vulnerable to water-related disease and death.
   D. developed countries manage their water supplies better than developing countries.

29. Sir Isaac Newton had the prescience to appreciate that his study of natural phenomena was of great import for the scientific community and for society as a whole. It is because of Newton's work that we currently understand the effect of gravity on the earth as a global system. As a result of Newton's investigation into the subject of gravity, we know today that geological features such as mountains and canyons can cause variances in the Earth's gravitational force. Newton must also be acknowledged for the realization that the force of gravity becomes less robust as the distance from the equator diminishes, due to the rotation of the earth, as well as the declining mass and density of the planet from the equator to the poles.

   What is the author's main purpose?
   A. to analyze natural phenomena
   B. to reconcile various gravitational theories
   C. to identify a reservation which Newton experienced
   D. to emphasize the significance of Newton's achievement

30. The corpus of research on Antarctica has resulted in an abundance of factual data. For example, we now know that more than ninety nine percent of the land is completely covered by snow and ice, making Antarctica the coldest continent on the planet. This inhospitable climate has brought about the adaptation of a plethora of plants and biological organisms present on the continent. An investigation into the sedimentary geological formations provides testimony to the process of adaptation. Sediments recovered from the bottom of Antarctic lakes, as well as bacteria discovered in ice, have revealed the history of climate change over the past 10,000 years.

According to the passage, the plants and organisms in Antarctica
   A.   have survived because of the process of adaptation.
   B.   are the result of sedimentary geological formations.
   C.   cover more than 99% of the land surface.
   D.   grow in the bottom of lakes on the continent.

31. *For the following ten questions, you will see two sentences. Read the sentences, and then choose the best answer to the question.*

The dangers of smoking have been reported widely in the media in recent years.

Increasing numbers of teenagers are beginning to take up smoking every year.

How are the two sentences related?
   A.   They repeat the same idea.
   B.   They give a problem and solution.
   C.   They provide a general rule and a specific example.
   D.   They create a contrast.

32. Last month, the city established a neighborhood watch scheme because of a spate of home burglaries.

House break-ins have fallen dramatically in the city this month.

What does the second sentence do?
   A.   It states the effect.
   B.   It gives an example.
   C.   It offers a solution.
   D.   It makes a comparison.

33. Driving a car is a skill that is easily acquired.

Many would-be motorists report that their driving lessons are arduous and exacting.

How are the two sentences related?
   A.   They present problems and solutions. x
   B.   They contradict one another.
   C.   They give a cause and its effect.
   D.   They provide explanations for a contentious topic.

34. Certain well-publicized studies have indicated that prolonged cell phone use can lead to cancer in the brain.

Increasing numbers of people are purchasing and using cell phones every year, in spite of the potential health risks.

What does the second sentence do?
   A. It exemplifies the first sentence.
   B. It explains the reason for the result mentioned in the first sentence.
   C. It gives unexpected information.
   D. It draws a conclusion about what is stated in the first sentence.

35. International students require proficiency in the English language if they are to be successful at American colleges and universities.

In order to thrive academically, non-native speakers of English attending tertiary educational institutions in the United States need advanced English language skills.

What does the second sentence do?
   A. It restates the claim made in first sentence.
   B. It sums up the points raised in the first sentence.
   C. It provides an example for what is stated in the first sentence.
   D. It gives unexpected information.

36. The use of technology in our lives can negatively influence social relationships because people rely less on face-to-face communication.

Many communities have instituted more frequent local events in order to increase opportunities for social interaction and open dialogue among their residents.

What does the second sentence do?
   A. It repeats the same idea as stated in the first sentence.
   B. It contradicts the evidence given in the first sentence.
   C. It provides an application for the theory provided in the first sentence.
   D. It presents a solution to the problem mentioned in the first sentence.

37. Poverty adversely affects the youngest children of society to the greatest extent, particularly in the areas of health and welfare.

Infants and toddlers from low income families often do not receive essential social and medical services because their parents cannot afford to pay for them.

What does the second sentence do?
   A. It supports the point stated in the first sentence.
   B. It presents a solution to the problem mentioned in the first sentence.
   C. It provides a general application of the specific example given in the first sentence.
   D. It contradicts the idea as stated in the first sentence.

38. Astrology is at best to be regarded as an ill-founded pseudo-science.

Modern day astrologists sometimes struggle to keep up with increasing numbers of requests for their services.

How are the two sentences related?
   A. They reinforce each other.
   B. They provide a contrast.
   C. They repeat the same idea.
   D. The second analyzes the claim made in the first.

39. It is widely believed that dinosaurs became extinct as a consequence of a catastrophic meteorological event.

Archeological evidence recovered near the Gulf of Mexico demonstrates that dinosaurs died out after a large asteroid struck the area.

What does the second sentence do?
   A. It repeats the same idea as stated in the first sentence.
   B. It refutes the point raised in the first sentence.
   C. It presents a solution to the problem mentioned in the first sentence.
   D. It analyzes the claim made in the first sentence.

40. The law of perpetual motion states that objects in motion will remain in motion.

Once a vehicle has gained momentum, it will stop only if the brakes are applied.

What does the second sentence do?
   A. It applies the theory mentioned in the first sentence.
   B. It restates the theory mentioned in the first sentence.
   C. It gives a solution to the problem described in the first sentence.
   D. It contradicts the evidence provided in the first sentence.

41. *Solve the seventeen following arithmetic problems and select the correct answer from the choices given. You may use paper to work out your answers.*

$5.25 + .003 + .428 = ?$
   A. 9.533
   B. 5.708
   C. 5.681
   D. 0.956

42. $7.22 \times 2.5 = ?$
   A. 0.18050
   B. 1.8050
   C. 18.050
   D. 180.50

9

43. Three people are going to give money to a famous charity. Person J will provide one-half of the money. Person K will donate one-eighth of the money. What fraction represents Person L's contribution of money to the charity?
   A. 2/8
   B. 3/8
   C. 5/8
   D. 3/16

44. Which of the following is the least?
   A. .28
   B. .028
   C. .208
   D. .82

45. 8/50 = ?
   A. 0.16
   B. 1.6
   C. .625
   D. 6.25

46. 80 is 25 percent of what number?
   A. 20
   B. 160
   C. 200
   D. 320

47. 5/6 – 1/3 = ?
   A. 1/2
   B. 1/3
   C. 1/4
   D. 5/18

48. 7¾ – 3½ = ?
   A. 4½
   B. 4¼
   C. 3¼
   D. 3¾

49. Which of the following is the closest to 14.1 × 4.9 ?
   A. 56
   B. 60
   C. 70
   D. 75

50. All of the following are correct ways to write 20 percent of y except:
   A. 20y/100
   B. y/5
   C. .20y
   D. 20y

51. A basketball team had 60 games this season and lost 40 percent of them. How many games did the team win?
      A. 12
      B. 24
      C. 36
      D. 40

52. $144 \div 32 = ?$
      A. .222222
      B. 4.5
      C. 22.2222
      D. 45

53. $7.55 + .055 + .02 = ?$
      A. 7.625
      B. 7.805
      C. 8.12
      D. 75.575

54. 1/8 is equivalent to which percentage?
      A. 0.125%
      B. 1.25%
      C. 12.5%
      D. 25%

55. Which of the following is closest to $402 \div 7.8$?
      A. 50
      B. 57
      C. 58
      D. 62

56. Jack took a math test that had 50 questions. He got 10% of his answers wrong. How many questions did he answer correctly?
      A. 5
      B. 10
      C. 40
      D. 45

57. Which of the following is the greatest?
      A. .390
      B. .039
      C. .0935
      D. .5093

58. *Solve the twelve following algebra problems and select the correct answer from the choices given. You may use paper to work out your answers.*

$(-13 + 5) \div 2 = ?$
   A. 2
   B. −2
   C. 4
   D. −4

59. $(x^2 - 4) \div (x - 2) = ?$
   A. $x + 2$
   B. $x - 2$
   C. $x^2 + x - 2$
   D. $x^2 + x - 4$

60. If $4x - 3(x + 2) = -3$, then $x = ?$
   A. 2
   B. −2
   C. 3
   D. −3

61. $(3x + 2y)^2 = ?$
   A. $9x^2 + 4y^2$
   B. $9x^2 + 4y^2 + 12xy$
   C. $9x^2 - 4y^2$
   D. $9x^2 + 4y^2 - 12xy$

62. $(2x - 2y)(x + 3y) = ?$
   A. $2x^2 + 8xy - 6y^2$
   B. $2x^2 + 8xy + 6y^2$
   C. $2x^2 + 4xy - 6y^2$
   D. $2x^2 + 4xy + 6y^2$

63. What is the value of the expression $5x^2 - 2xy + y^2$ when $x = 3$ and $y = -3$?
   A. −36
   B. 19
   C. 35
   D. 72

64. Two people are going to work on a project. The first person will be paid $10.25 per hour. The second person will be paid $12.50 per hour. If A represents the number of hours the first person will work, and B represents the number of hours the second person will work, which equation below represents the total cost of the wages for this job?
   A. A + B
   B. 22.75(A + B)
   C. (10.25 x A) + (12.50 x B)
   D. (12.50 x A) + (10.25 x B)

65. If a circle A has a radius of 3, what is the circumference of the circle?
  A. 3π
  B. 6π
  C. 9π
  D. $9\pi/2$

66. $4^5 \times 4^2 = ?$
  A. 4^3
  B. 4^7
  C. 4^{10}
  D. 16^7

67. $30 - \frac{3}{4}X > 27$, then $X <$
  A. $X < 3$
  B. $X < -3$
  C. $X < -4$
  D. $X < 4$

68. $-4(5 - 2) - 3(4 - 6) = ?$
  A. -6
  B. 6
  C. -18
  D. 18

69. $\sqrt{11} \times \sqrt{3} = ?$
  A. $\sqrt{33}$
  B. $\sqrt{14}$
  C. 33
  D. 14

70. *Solve the twenty following college-level math problems and select the correct answer from the choices given. You may use paper to work out your answers.*

  $3xy - 9x^2y + 12y^2x^2 = ?$
  A. $xy(1 - 3x + 4xy)$
  B. $3xy(1 - 3x + 4xy)$
  C. $xy(1 + 3x + 4xy)$
  D. $-3xy(1 + 3x + 4xy)$

71. $(x + 2) - (x^2 - x) = ?$
  A. $2x - x^2$
  B. $2x + x^2 - 2$
  C. $2x + x^2 + 2$
  D. $2x - x^2 + 2$

72. 3, 6, 12, 24

     What number is next in the sequence?
     A. 30
     B. 36
     C. 48
     D. 54

73. $3^7 \div 3^4 = ?$
    A. 1^3
    B. 3^3
    C. 3^{11}
    D. 3^{28}

74. $\dfrac{x^2+10x+16}{x^2+11x+18} \times \dfrac{x^2+9x}{x^2+17x+72} = ?$

    A. $\dfrac{9}{x+9}$

    B. $\dfrac{x}{x+9}$

    C. $\dfrac{x^2}{x^2+17x}$

    D. $\dfrac{x+1}{x+8}$

75. A train travels at 120 miles per hour. The train is currently 270 miles from Chicago. How long will it take for the train to arrive in Chicago?
    A. 45 minutes
    B. 2 hours and 15 minutes
    C. 2 hours and 25 minutes
    D. 2 hours and 45 minutes

76. How many 4 letter permutations can be made from the letter set: K I T E S?
    A. 120
    B. 100
    C. 60
    D. 9

77. If $x - 2 > 0$ and $y = x - 2$, then
    A. $y > 0$
    B. $y > 2$
    C. $y < 0$
    D. $y = 0$

14

78. What is the determinant of the following matrix:

$$\begin{bmatrix} w & x \\ y & z \end{bmatrix}$$

    A. $wz + xy$
    B. $wx + yz$
    C. $wz - xy$
    D. $wx - yz$

79. Find the coordinates (x, y) of the midpoint of the line segment on a graph that connects the points (–6, 2) and (2, –6).
    A. (–2, 2)
    B. (2, –2)
    C. (–2, –2)
    D. (2, 2)

80. $\sqrt{5b - 4} = 4$
   What is the value of b?
    A. 0
    B. $^5/_4$
    C. 4
    D. an imaginary number

81. Consider a two-dimensional linear graph where $x = 4$ and $y = 12$. The line crosses the y axis at 2. What is the slope of this line?
    A. .33
    B. 3.5
    C. 2.0
    D. 2.5

82. If $2 + 4(2\sqrt{x} + 2) = 26,$ then $\sqrt{x} = ?$
    A. 2
    B. $\sqrt{2}$
    C. $\sqrt{8}$
    D. 128

83. Which one of the following ordered pairs is a solution to the following system of equations?

$x + y = 8$
$xy = 15$
    A. (1, 15)
    B. (8, 15)
    C. (3, 5)
    D. (2, 4)

84. *ai* and *ci* are imaginary numbers. *b* and *d* are real numbers. When does $ai - b = ci - d$?
   A. Only if $a = b$ and $c = d$
   B. Only if $a = c$ and $b = d$
   C. Only if $a = b$ and $c = d$
   D. Only if $a = d$ and $b = c$

85. Consider a right-angled triangle, where side X and side Y form the right angle, and side Z is the hypotenuse. If X = 2 and Y = 5, what is the length of side Z?
   A. $\sqrt{7}$
   B. 7
   C. 29
   D. $\sqrt{29}$

86. $5^3 = 125$ is equal to which of the following?
   A. $125 = \log_5 3$
   B. $125 = \log_3 5$
   C. $5 = \log_3 125$
   D. $3 = \log_5 125$

87. $x^{-5} = ?$
   A. $-1 \times x^5$
   B. $1 \div x^5$
   C. $-1 + x^5$
   D. $-1 - x^5$

88. Use the quadratic formula to solve: $x^2 - 4x - 8 = 0$
   A. $2 \pm 2\sqrt{3}$
   B. $2 + 2\sqrt{3}$
   C. $2 - 2\sqrt{3}$
   D. $4 \pm 4\sqrt{3}$

89. For the following equation, i represents an imaginary number: $(6 - 3i) - (-2 - i) = ?$
   A. $4 - 4i$
   B. $8 - 4i$
   C. $8 - 2i$
   D. $8 + 2i$

ACCUPLACER PRACTICE TEST 1 – ANSWERS

1. The correct answer is D. The clause *Although she was only sixteen years old* modifies the pronoun "she." Therefore, "she" needs to come after this clause.

2. The correct answer is A. This question is an example of the inverted sentence structure. When a sentence begins with a negative phrase [no sooner, not only, never, etc.], the past perfect tense [had + past participle] must be used. In addition, the auxiliary verb "had" must be placed *in front of* the grammatical subject of the sentence [I].

3. The correct answer is B. This question is about "parallelism." In order to follow the grammatical rules of parallelism, you must be sure that all of the items you give in a list are of the same part of speech. So, all of the items must be nouns or verbs, for example. In other words, you should not use both nouns and verbs in a list. Answer B has all nouns, but the other answer choices have some nouns and some verbs.

4. The correct answer is D. This question is about the use of punctuation. "However, the noise next door made it impossible" is a complete sentence. It has a grammatical subject [the noise] and a verb [made]. "However" must be preceded by a period, and the new sentence must begin with a capital letter. In addition, "however" is a sentence linker. So "however" must be followed with a comma.

5. The correct answer is A. The words "which would be spacious enough to transport her equipment" form a restrictive modifier. A restrictive modifier is a clause or phrase that provides essential information about a noun in the sentence. In other words, we would not know exactly what kind of new car she wanted without the clause "which would be spacious enough to transport her equipment." Restrictive modifiers should not be preceded by a comma.

6. The correct answer is C. The prepositional phrase "Near a small river at the bottom of the canyon" describes the location of the people when they made their discovery. So the prepositional phrase must be followed by "we." Since the prepositional phrase is at the beginning of the sentence, the complete phrase needs to be followed with a comma. Note that you need to put in only *one* comma *at the end* of such prepositional phrases.

7. The correct answer is B. This question tests your knowledge of "who" and "whom." Remember to use "who" when the person you are talking about is doing the action, but to use "whom" when the person is receiving an action. In this sentence, the candidate is receiving the action of being selected. So the question should begin with "whom." The auxiliary verb "did" needs to come directly after "whom" to have the correct word order for this type of question.

8. The correct answer is A. The phrase "Always and Forever" is an example of a restrictive modifier. As mentioned in question number 5, restrictive modifiers are clauses or phrases that provide essential information in order to identify the subject. In other words, without the phrase "Always and Forever" in this sentence, we would not know exactly which song they played at their wedding. So the phrase conveys essential information. Note that restrictive modifiers should not be preceded by a comma.

9. The correct answer is B. In this sentence, the word "as" functions as a subordinating conjunction. Commas should not be placed before subordinating conjunctions. Other examples of subordinating conjunctions are "because" and "since."

10. The correct answer is C. If you are talking about yourself in an imaginary situation, you need to use *were* instead of *was*. This is known as the subjunctive mood. In the other half of the sentence, you need to use the verb "would" when you are describing and imaginary situation.

11. The correct answer is B. The new sentence would be constructed as follows: Even though she worked all night, she still did not finish the project. Sentences that begin with "even though" are used to introduce an unexpected result to a situation. Remember that "even though" is used to join subordinate clauses to sentences. Subordinate clauses contain a grammatical subject (she) and a verb (worked).

12. The correct answer is C. The new sentence would be constructed as follows: Despite snow showers being common in the north during the winter, precipitation is unlikely tomorrow. "Despite" takes a noun phrase, not a clause.

In other words, the part of the sentence that contains "despite" should not include a verb. "Despite" should also not be followed directly by "of." In this example, the word "being" functions as an adjectival phrase, not a verb.

13. The correct answer is D. The new sentence would be constructed as follows: Because it is warm all year round, Florida has many out-of-state visitors during December and January. "Because" is a subordinator. In other words, the part of the sentence that includes "because" also needs to include a verb. Answer D contains a verb [is], but the other answers do not have verbs.

14. The correct answer is A. The new sentence is: Just as Tom is highly intelligent, so too is his younger brother. Comparative sentences that begin with "just as" need to include "so too" in the other part of the sentence.

15. The correct answer is B. The new sentence is formed as follows: After Mary had arrived at the party, I decided to go home. Clauses that begin with "After" normally need to contain the past perfect tense. The past perfect tense is formed with "had" plus the past participle, which is "arrived" in this sentence.

16. The correct answer is C. "Provided" is used in sentences in the same way as "if." So in the above sentence, we can replace "if" with "provided." In addition, the end of the original sentence is moved to the beginning of the new sentence. Be sure you put a comma after the "if" clause once you have changed the sentence. The new sentence is: Provided you work hard, you will succeed at college.

17. The correct answer is B. The phrase "kind and patient" modifies the word "teacher." Therefore, your new sentence will be: Kind and patient, she is a good teacher.

18. The correct answer is A. The new sentence is constructed as follows: Besides being rude, she is also stingy. In sentences like this, you can just replace the phrase "apart from" with the word "besides."

19. The correct answer is D. The new sentence is: Because of the student's insolence, the teacher became upset. Remember that "because" is a subordinator. So "because" needs to be followed by a verb. On the other hand, "because of" is a phrase linker. So the part of the sentence that contains "because of" needs to be followed by a noun phrase. "The student's insolence" is a noun phrase.

20. The correct answer is C. The new sentence is: Increasing numbers of teenagers are developing type II diabetes. The word "increasing" needs to be followed by "numbers" or "amounts."

21. The correct answer is C. Misconception means misunderstanding. The phrase "as most people seem to believe" in the passage indicates that there as been a misunderstanding. The also passage provides information on a trend, but the *primary* purpose is to clear up a misunderstanding.

22. The correct answer is B. The phrase "results *like* the super tomato" indicates that the super tomato is only one example. The other ideas are not implied by the passage.

23. The correct answer is A. The passage describes how Lewis and Clark met and why they made their famous expedition together. The passage mentions Thomas Jefferson, but this is only a minor point of the passage. The passage does not defend the purchase, nor does it make any comparisons.

24. The correct answer is C. The key sentence is: "After making inquiries, the FBI discovered that this money originated from the Committee for the Re-election of the President, thereby confirming governmental involvement." This sentence signals the reason why the break in failed when it uses the

18

word "thereby." Answers A and D are mentioned in the passage, but they are not the reason for the failure. Answer B is not stated in the passage. Note that the subterfuge was part of the cover-up, not an action by the FBI.

25. The correct answer is D. The passage mentions both cost-effectiveness and benefits to the environment. In other words, answer D gives the main idea, but answers A, B, and C give specific information.

26. The correct answer is A. The passage states: "Indeed, research shows that there is a definite link between the consumption of high-fat food and cancer." So, conversely, we can understand that a low-fat diet will decrease the chances of getting cancer. The other answers are not implied in the passage.

27. The correct answer is C. The passage states that MI "is rapidly replacing . . . IQ." It also states that the IQ test "has come under criticism recently." Therefore, answer C gives the main idea. Answers A, B, and D are *specific* points from the passage.

28. The correct answer is B. The passage uses the phrases "people . . . die needlessly" and "fresh water saves lives." Therefore, it is the writer's viewpoint that the deaths could be avoided. The information in answers A, C, and D is not stated in the passage.

29. The correct answer is D. The passage uses the word "prescience," which means insight, to describe Newton in the topic sentence. Later, the writer uses the phrases "because of Newton's work . . . we currently understand" and "As a result of Newton's investigation . . . we know today." Therefore, the writer believes that Newton made a significant achievement.

30. The correct answer is A. The passage states: "This inhospitable climate has brought about the adaptation . . . "

31. The correct answer is D. If the dangers of smoking are well known, one would expect that fewer people would want to do it. However, in spite of the dangers, more and more teenagers are beginning to smoke. Therefore, the unexpected result in the second sentence creates a contrast with the statement made in the first sentence.

32. The correct answer is A. The break-ins have fallen because of the new scheme. Therefore, the reduction is the effect or the result of the scheme.

33. The correct answer is B. The phrase "easily acquired" mentioned in the first sentence opposes the idea of "arduous and exacting" (or difficult) mentioned in the second sentence. Therefore, the sentences contradict each other.

34. The correct answer is C. The first sentence mentions the problems associated with cell phones, namely their association with brain cancer. The second sentence talks about the increasing numbers of people who use cell phones, in spite of the dangers. We would expect the amount of people using cell phones to decrease, but the opposite has happened. In other words, this is an unexpected result.

35. The correct answer is A. "Thrive" means to be successful. "Proficiency" means advanced skills. Therefore, the sentences repeat the same idea.

36. The correct answer is D. The local events and social interaction mentioned in the second sentence are a solution to the problem of negatively-influenced social relationships mentioned in the first sentence.

37. The correct answer is A. The first sentence makes a general point about children and poverty, which is supported by the specific idea about infants and toddlers in the second sentence.

38. The correct answer is B. The phrase "ill-founded pseudo-science" indicates that the writer has a very low opinion of astrology. Despite some people having this kind of low opinion, we learn in the second sentence that there is an ever-increasing demand for astrologists. Therefore, the sentences contrast each other.

39. The correct answer is D. The first sentence makes a limited claim by using the phrase "it is widely believed." The second sentence expands on the first one because the recovered evidence demonstrates that there was a catastrophic event, i.e., the asteroid. The second sentence is much more specific than the first one, so we cannot say that they repeat the same idea.

40. The correct answer is A. The second sentence deals only with one vehicle, not all objects. So the second sentence applies the rule mentioned in the first sentence to one specific situation. Therefore, we cannot say that the sentences restate the same idea.

41. The correct answer is C. When you add, be sure to line all of the decimals up in a column:

```
5.250
0.003
0.428
5.681
```

As you can see, you should add zeros where necessary at the beginning or end of the numbers in order to make the decimal points line up.

42. The correct answer is C. Be sure to put the decimal point in the correct position after you do the long multiplication. We know that the decimal point has to be three places from the right on the final product because 7.22 has 2 decimal places and 2.5 has 1 decimal place, so 1 plus 2 equals 3 places.

```
   7.22
×  2.5
  3.610
 14.440
 18.050
```

43. The correct answer is B. The sum of contributions from all three people must be equal to 100%, simplified to 1. In other words, they make up the whole donation by contributing together:

$$J + K + L = 1$$
$$1/2 + 1/8 + L = 1$$

Now, find the lowest common denominator of the fractions:

$$4/8 + 1/8 + L = 1$$
$$5/8 + L = 1$$
$$L = 1 - 5/8$$
$$L = 3/8$$

44. The correct answer is B. Line all of the decimal points up for problems like this. Put in zeros where necessary, as follows:

0.280
0.028
0.208
0.820

When you have them lined up like this, you can see that 0.028 is the smallest one.

45. The correct answer is A. You must do long division until you have no remainder:

```
      .16
50) 8.00
     .50
     .30
     .30
       0
```

46. The correct answer is D. 25 percent is equal to 0.25. The phrase "of what number" indicates that we need to divide the two amounts given in the problem: $80 \div 0.25 = 320$.

We can check this result as follows: $320 \times 0.25 = 80$

47. The correct answer is A. In fraction problems like this, you have to find the lowest common denominator. [The denominator is the number on the bottom of the fraction.] In other words, before you subtract the fractions, you have to change them so that the bottom numbers for each fraction are the same, in this case, sixths. You do this by multiplying the numerator [top number] by the same number you use on the denominator:

$1/3 \times 2/2 = 2/6$

When you have got both fractions in the same denominator, you subtract them:

$5/6 - 2/6 = 3/6$
$3/6 = 1/2$

48. The correct answer is B. Questions like this test your knowledge of mixed numbers. Mixed numbers are those that contain a whole number and a fraction. If the fraction on the first mixed number is greater than the fraction on the second mixed number, you can subtract the whole numbers and the fractions separately. Remember to use the lowest common denominator on the fractions:

$7 - 3 = 4$

$3/4 - 1/2 =$
$3/4 - 2/4 = 1/4$

Therefore, the result is 4¼.

49. The correct answer is C. For estimation problems like this, round the decimals up or down to the nearest whole number. 14.1 is rounded down to 14, and 4.9 is rounded up to 5. Then do long multiplication:

```
   14
×   5
─────
   70
```

50. You should choose answer D. This question tests your knowledge of how to express percentages. Percentages can always be expressed as that number over one hundred. So 20% = 20/100. Therefore, answer A is correct. Percentages can also be simplified from their fractions. In order to simplify the fraction, you have to find the largest number that will go into both the numerator and denominator.

In this case, the numerator and denominator are both divisible by 20. To simplify the numerator: 20 ÷ 20 = 1. To simplify the denominator: 100 ÷ 20 = 5. This results in the simplified fraction of 1/5. So answer B is also correct.

Percentages can also be expressed as decimals: 20% = 20/100 = 20 ÷ 100 = 0.20. Therefore, answer C is also correct.

Answer D is incorrect because it does not have a decimal point. So you must choose answer D.

51. The correct answer is C. For this problem, you must do long multiplication to determine how many games the team won. *However: Be careful!* The question tells you the percentage of games the team *lost*, not *won*. So, first of all, we have to calculate the percentage of games won. If the team lost 40 percent of the games, we know that the team won the remaining 60 percent.

Now do the long multiplication:

```
    60
×  .60
──────
 36.00
```

52. The correct answer is B. You must do long division until you have no remainder.

```
        4.5
32) 144.0
    128.0
     16.0
     16.0
        0
```

53. The correct answer is A. Remember to line up the decimal points as follows:

```
7.550
0.055
0.020
7.625
```

54. The correct answer is C.

$1 \div 8 = 0.125$

$0.125 = 12.5\%$

55. The correct answer is A. For estimation problems like this, round the numbers up or down to the nearest whole number.

402 is rounded down to 400, and 7.8 is rounded up to 8.

Then divide: $400 \div 8 = 50$

56. The correct answer is D. You must first determine the percentage of questions that Jack answered correctly. We know that he got 10% of the answers wrong, so therefore the remaining 90% were correct. Now we multiply the total number of questions by the percentage of correct answers:

$50 \times 90\% = 45$

57. The correct answer is D. Remember to put in zeros and line up the decimal points when you compare the numbers.

0.3900
0.0390
0.0935
0.5093

Therefore, the largest number is .5093

58. The correct answer is D. Deal with the part of the equation inside the parentheses first:

$(-13 + 5) \div 2 =$
$-8 \div 2$

Then do the division:

$-8 \div 2 = -4$

59. The correct answer is A.

$$
\begin{array}{r}
x + 2 \\
x - 2 \overline{)x^2 - 4} \\
\underline{x^2 - 2x} \\
2x - 4 \\
\underline{2x - 4} \\
0
\end{array}
$$

60. The correct answer is C. To solve this type of problem, do the multiplication on the items in parentheses first:

$4x - 3(x + 2) = -3$
$4x - 3x - 6 = -3$

Then deal with the integers by putting them on one side of the equation as follows:

$4x - 3x - 6 + 6 = -3 + 6$
$4x - 3x = 3$

Then solve for x:

$4x - 3x = 3$
$1x = 3$
$x = 3$

61. The correct answer is B.

$(3x + 2y)^2 =$
$(3x + 2y)(3x + 2y)$

This type of algebraic expression is known as a polynomial. When multiplying polynomials, you should use the F-O-I-L method. F-O-I-L means that you multiply the terms two at a time from each of the two parts of the equation in this order: First - Outside - Inside – Last.

FIRST: $3x \times 3x = 9x^2$
OUTSIDE: $3x \times 2y = 6xy$
INSIDE: $2y \times 3x = 6xy$
LAST: $2y \times 2y = 4y^2$

Then we add all of the above parts together to get:

$9x^2 + 4y^2 + 6xy + 6xy =$
$9x^2 + 4y^2 + 12xy$

62. The correct answer is C. Remember to use the F-O-I-L method when you multiply:

FIRST: $2x \times x = 2x^2$
OUTSIDE: $2x \times 3y = 6xy$
INSIDE: $-2y \times x = -2xy$
LAST: $-2y \times 3y = -y^2$

Then add all of the above once you have completed F-O-I-L:

$2x^2 + 6xy + -2xy + -6y^2 =$
$2x^2 + 6xy - 2xy - 6y^2 =$
$2x^2 + 4xy - 6y^2$

63. The correct answer is D. To solve this problem, put in the values for *x* and *y* and multiply. Remember to be careful when multiplying negative numbers:

$5x^2 - 2xy + y^2 =$
$(5 \times 3^2) - 2(3 \times -3) + (-3^2) =$
$(5 \times 3 \times 3) - (2 \times -9) + (-3 \times -3) =$
$(5 \times 9) - (2 \times -9) + (9) =$
$45 - (-18) + 9 =$
$45 + 18 + 8 = 72$

64. The correct answer is C. The two people are working at different per hour costs, so each person needs to have its own variable: A for the number of hours for the first person and B for the number of hours for the second person.

So the equation for wages for the first person is: (10.25 x A)
The equation for the wages for the second person is: (12.50 x B)

The total cost of the wages for this job is the sum of the wages of these two people:

(10.25 x A) + (12.50 x B)

65. The correct answer is B.

The circumference of a circle is always: π times the diameter.

The diameter of a circle is always equal to the radius times 2.

So, the diameter for this circle is 3 x 2 = 6 Therefore, the circumference is 6π

66. The correct answer is B. This question tests your knowledge of exponent laws. First look to see whether your base number is the same on each part of the equation. (4 is the base number for each part of this equation.) If the base number is the same, and the problem asks you to multiply, you simply add the exponents:

$4^5 \times 4^2 = 4^{5+2} = 4^7$

NOTE: If the base number is the same, and the problem asks you to *divide*, you *subtract* the exponents.

67. The correct answer is D. Deal with the whole numbers on each side of the equation first:

$30 - \frac{3}{4}X > 27 =$
$(30 - 30) - \frac{3}{4}X > (27 - 30) =$
$-\frac{3}{4}X > -3$

Then deal with the fraction:

$-\frac{3}{4}X > -3 =$
$4 \times -\frac{3}{4}X > -3 \times 4 =$
$-3X > -12$

Then deal with the remaining whole numbers:

$-3X > -12 =$
$-3X \div 3 > -12 \div 3 =$
$-X > -4$

Then, deal with the negative number:

$-X > -4 =$
$-X + 4 > -4 + 4 =$
$-X + 4 > 0$

Finally, isolate the unknown variable as a positive number:

$-X + 4 > 0 =$
$-X + X + 4 > 0 + X =$
$4 > X =$
$X < 4$

68. The correct answer is A. Complete the operations inside the parentheses first. Remember to be careful when multiplying the negative numbers:

$-4(5 - 2) - 3(4 - 6) =$
$-4(3) - 3(-2) =$
$(-4 \times 3) - (3 \times -2) =$
$-12 + 6 =$
-6

69. The correct answer is A. If you are asked to multiply two square roots, multiply the numbers inside the square roots: $11 \times 3 = 33$

Then put this result inside a square root symbol for your answer: $\sqrt{33}$

70. The correct answer is B. This type of question tests your knowledge of factoring. In order to factor an equation, you must figure out what variables are common to each term of the equation. Let's look at this equation: $3xy - 9x^2y + 12y^2x^2$

We can see that each term contains x. We can also see that each term contains y. So, now let's factor out xy: $3xy - 9x^2y + 12y^2x^2 = xy(3 - 9x + 12yx)$

Then, think about integers. We can see that all of the terms inside the parentheses are divisible by 3. Now let's factor out the 3. In order to do this, we divide each term inside the parentheses by 3:

$xy(3 - 9x + 12yx) = 3xy(1 - 3x + 4yx) = 3xy(1 - 3x + 4xy)$

71. The correct answer is D. This question is asking you to simplify the terms in the parentheses. First, you should look to see if there is any subtraction or if any of the numbers are negative. In this problem, the second part of the equation is subtracted. So we need to do the operation on the second set of parentheses first.

$(x + 2) - (x^2 - x) =$
$x + 2 - x^2 + x$

Now simplify for the common terms:

$x + 2 - x^2 + x =$
$x + x + 2 - x^2 =$
$2x + 2 - x^2 =$
$2x - x^2 + 2$

72. The correct answer is C. For questions like this one, try to find the pattern of relationship between the numbers. Here, we can see that:

$3 \times 2 = 6$
$6 \times 2 = 12$
$12 \times 2 = 24$

In other words, the next number in the sequence is always double the previous number.

$24 \times 2 = 48$

73. The correct answer is B. This question tests your knowledge of exponent laws. First look to see whether your base number is the same on each part of the equation. (3 is the base number for each part of this equation.) If the base number is the same, and the problem asks you to divide, you simply subtract the exponents:

$3^7 \div 3^4 = 3^{7-4} = 3^3$

74. The correct answer is B. For this type of problem, first you need to find the factors of the numerators and denominators of each fraction.

$$\frac{x^2 + 10x + 16}{x^2 + 11x + 18} = \frac{(x+2)(x+8)}{(x+2)(x+9)} \qquad \frac{x^2 + 9x}{x^2 + 17x + 72} = \frac{x(x+9)}{(x+8)(x+9)}$$

Then for each fraction, you need to simplify by removing the common factors.

$$\frac{(x+2)(x+8)}{(x+2)(x+9)} = \frac{(x+8)}{(x+9)} \qquad \frac{x(x+9)}{(x+8)(x+9)} = \frac{x}{(x+8)}$$

Once you have simplified each fraction, perform the operation indicated. In this problem, you need to multiply the two fractions.

$$\frac{(x+8)}{(x+9)} \times \frac{x}{(x+8)} = \frac{x(x+8)}{(x+9)(x+8)}$$

When you have completed the operation, you need to check to see whether any further simplification is possible, In this case, the fraction may be further simplified because the numerator and denominator share the common factor $(x + 8)$.

$$\frac{x(x+8)}{(x+9)(x+8)} = \frac{x}{x+9}$$

75. The correct answer is B. Remember to read questions like this one very carefully. If the train travels at 120 miles an hour and needs to go 270 more miles, we need to divide the miles to travel by the miles per hour:

miles to travel ÷ miles per hour = time remaining

So, if we substitute the values from the question, we get: 270 ÷ 120 = 2.25

One hour contains 60 minutes, so 60 x .25 = 15 minutes. In other words, the total time is 2 hours and 15 minutes.

76. The correct answer is A. Permutations are like combinations, except permutations take into account the order of the items in each group. In order to calculate the number of permutations of size S taken from N items, you should use this formula: $N! \div (N - S)!$

For the question above: $N = 5$ and $S = 4$

$N! \div (N - S)! =$
$(5 \times 4 \times 3 \times 2 \times 1) \div (5 - 4) =$
$(5 \times 4 \times 3 \times 2) \div 1 =$
$120 \div 1 = 120$

77. The correct answer is A. This is an inequality problem. Notice that both equations contain $x - 2$. Therefore, we can substitute y for $x - 2$ in the first equation:

$x - 2 > 0$
$x - 2 = y$
$y > 0$

78. The correct answer is C. In order to find the determinant for a two-by-two matrix, you need to cross multiply and then subtract:

$$\begin{bmatrix} w & x \\ y & z \end{bmatrix}$$

So w is multiplied by z and y is multiplied by x.

Then we subtract the two terms to get the determinant: $wz - yx = wz - xy$

79. The correct answer is C. This question covers coordinate geometry. Remember that in order to find midpoints on a line, you need to use the midpoint formula. For two points on a graph (x_1, y_1) and (x_2, y_2), the midpoint is: $(x_1 + x_2) \div 2 , (y_1 + y_2) \div 2$

Now calculate for x and y:

$(-6 + 2) \div 2 =$ midpoint x, $(2 + -6) \div 2 =$ midpoint y
$-4 \div 2 =$ midpoint x, $-4 \div 2 =$ midpoint y
$-2 =$ midpoint x, $-2 =$ midpoint y

80. The correct answer is C. In order to find the value of a variable inside a square root sign, your first step is to square each side of the equation.

$$\sqrt{(5b - 4)^2} = 4^2$$
$$5b - 4 = 16$$

Then get the integers on one side of the equation:

$$5b - 4 = 16$$
$$5b - 4 + 4 = 16 + 4$$
$$5b = 20$$

Then isolate the variable to one side of the equation in order to solve the problem.

$$5b \div 5 = 20 \div 5$$
$$b = 4$$

81. The correct answer is D. In order to calculate the slope of a line, you need the slope-intercept formula: $y = mx + b$

NOTE: m is the slope and b is the y intercept (the point at which the line crosses the y axis).
Now solve for the numbers given in the problem:

$y = mx + b$
$12 = m4 + 2$
$12 - 2 = m4 + 2 - 2$
$10 = m4$
$10 \div 4 = m4 \div 4$
$2.5 = m$

82. The correct answer is A. In equations that have both integers and square roots, deal with the integers that are outside the parentheses:

$$2 + 4(2\sqrt{x} + 2) = 26$$
$$2 + 8\sqrt{x} + 8 = 26$$
$$10 + 8\sqrt{x} = 26$$
$$10 - 10 + 8\sqrt{x} = 26 - 10$$
$$8\sqrt{x} = 16$$

Then divide:

$$8\sqrt{x} = 16$$
$$(8\sqrt{x}) \div 8 = 16 \div 8$$
$$\sqrt{x} = 2$$

83. The correct answer is C. For questions on systems of equations like this one, you should look at the multiplication equation first. Ask yourself, what are the factors of 15?

We know that 15 is the product of the following:

$1 \times 15 = 15$
$3 \times 5 = 15$

Now add each of the two factors together to solve the first equation:

$1 + 15 = 16$
$3 + 5 = 8$

(3, 5) solves both equations. Therefore, it is the correct answer.

84. The correct answer is B. Two complex numbers are equal if and only if their real parts are equal and their imaginary parts are equal. Therefore, a must be equal to c and b must be equal to d.

85. The correct answer is D. The length of the hypotenuse is always the square root of the sum of the squares of the other two sides of the triangle:

hypotenuse length $Z = \sqrt{X^2 + Y^2}$

Now put in the values for the above problem:

$$Z = \sqrt{X^2 + Y^2}$$
$$Z = \sqrt{2^2 + 5^2}$$
$$Z = \sqrt{4 + 25}$$
$$Z = \sqrt{29}$$

86. The correct answer is D. Logarithmic functions are just another way of expressing exponents. Remember that $y^x = Z$ is always the same as $x = \log_y Z$.

87. The correct answer is B. Remember that a negative exponent is always equal to 1 divided by the variable. Therefore, $x^{-5} = 1 \div x^5$

88. The correct answer is A. For any equation in the form $ax^2 \pm bx \pm c = 0$, the quadratic formula is as follows:

$$x = (-b \pm \sqrt{b^2 - 4ac}) \div 2a$$

Now put in the values from the equation given in the question, and solve for x. For $x^2 - 4x - 8 = 0$

a = 1
b = –4
c = –8

So, we put these in the quadratic formula:

$$(-b \pm \sqrt{b^2 - 4ac}) \div 2a =$$
$$(--4 \pm \sqrt{-4^2 - 4ac}) \div 2a =$$
$$(4 \pm \sqrt{16 - 4(1 \times -8)} \div (2 \times 1) =$$
$$(4 \pm \sqrt{16 + 32}) \div 2 =$$
$$(4 \pm \sqrt{48}) \div 2$$

Now find the squared factors of the number inside the square root sign.

48 = 3 × 16

Note: We use 16 because it is the square of 4.

$$(4 \pm \sqrt{3 \times 16}) \div 2 =$$
$$(4 \pm 4\sqrt{3}) \div 2 =$$
$$2 \pm 2\sqrt{3}$$

89. The correct answer is C. To solve this type of problem, do the operations on the parentheses first.

(6 – 3i) – (– 2 – i) = 6 – 3i + 2 + i

Then group the real and imaginary numbers together:

6 – 3i + 2 + i =
6 + 2 – 3i + i =
8 – 2i

1. *Select the best substitute for the underlined parts of the following ten sentences. The first answer [choice A] is identical to the original sentence. If you think the original sentence is best, then choose A as your answer.*

   The child tried to grab the cookies from the <u>shelf, however they were</u> out of reach.
   - A. shelf, however they were
   - B. shelf: however they were
   - C. shelf. However, they were
   - D. shelf however, they were

2. Covered in chocolate <u>frosting, the hostess dropped the cake</u> in front of all her guests.
   - A. frosting, the hostess dropped the cake
   - B. frosting, the hostess cake dropped
   - C. frosting, the cake was dropped by the hostess
   - D. frosting, by the hostess the cake was dropped

3. <u>To love and be loved</u> is the greatest happiness of existence.
   - A. To love and be loved
   - B. Loving and be loved
   - C. Loving and to be loved
   - D. To love and being loved

4. He wanted to buy a <u>telescope, one which he could</u> use to gaze at the stars.
   - A. telescope, one which he could
   - B. telescope, which one he could
   - C. telescope one which he could
   - D. telescope. One which he could

5. No sooner <u>I had finished gardening than</u> it began to rain.
   - A. I had finished the gardening than
   - B. I finished the gardening than
   - C. had I finished the gardening
   - D. had finished I the gardening than

6. If <u>I went out</u> alone after dark, I try to be more alert and careful.
   - A. I went out
   - B. I go out
   - C. I had gone out
   - D. I were going out

7. "I am not really interested in <u>this movie" he</u> said.
   - A. this movie" he
   - B. this movie," he
   - C. this movie" . he
   - D. this movie." He

8. When a person is confused about his or her identity, this is known as an identity crisis.
    A. When a person is confused about his or her identity, this
    B. When you are confused about your identity, this
    C. The experience of confusion about one's own identity, this
    D. The experience of confusion about one's own identity

9. Upset, from receiving the bad news, Mary broke down and cried.
    A. Upset, from receiving the bad news, Mary
    B. Upset, from receiving the bad news Mary
    C. Upset from receiving the bad news, Mary
    D. Upset from receiving the bad news Mary,

10. Dilapidated and disheveled the house appeared forlorn and abandoned.
    A. Dilapidated and disheveled the house appeared
    B. Dilapidated and disheveled the house, appeared
    C. Dilapidated and disheveled the house appeared,
    D. Dilapidated and disheveled, the house appeared

11. *Rewrite the following ten sentences mentally in your own head. Follow the directions given for the formation of the new sentence. Remember that your new sentence should be grammatically correct and convey the same meaning as the original sentence.*

    She wanted that new car for so long, and when she finally got it, she was so excited. Rewrite, beginning with: She was excited because she

    Your new sentence will include:
    A. wanting that new car
    B. that new car, which
    C. that new car which
    D. which she finally got

12. It will be easy to pass my math test, but I cannot say the same about my physics test. Rewrite, beginning with: Unlike my physics test,

    The next words will be:
    A. it will be easy
    B. I should easily
    C. my math test
    D. passing math

13. She felt ill for days and eventually came down with the flu. Rewrite, beginning with: Having felt

    Your new sentence will include:
    A. daily illness
    B. eventually down she came
    C. the flu eventually came
    D. she eventually came down

14. If she could afford it, she would come to Hawaii with us. Rewrite, beginning with: <u>She is not able to come to Hawaii with us</u>

    The next words will be:
    - A. because she
    - B. without her
    - C. although there
    - D. without enough

15. The referee blew his whistle, and then the game began. Rewrite, beginning with: <u>The game began</u>

    The next words will be:
    - A. the referee blowing
    - B. and the referee
    - C. after the referee
    - D. although the referee

16. Thomas studied extensively for his final exams, but Mary did not do likewise. Rewrite, beginning with: <u>Whereas Thomas</u>

    Your new sentence will include:
    - A. unlike Mary
    - B. Mary did not
    - C. Mary did too
    - D. so did Mary

17. He will only get the promotion if he receives approval from his superiors. Rewrite, beginning with: <u>Unless he receives approval from his superiors,</u>

    The next words will be:
    - A. the promotion will be
    - B. he will be
    - C. he will get
    - D. he will not get

18. In spite of giving her best effort, Barbara failed to complete the project on time. Rewrite, beginning with: <u>Although</u>

    The next words will be:
    - A. she gave
    - B. her effort
    - C. her giving
    - D. she failed completing

19. Sarah's father was a foreign diplomat, so she has lived in many locations around the world. Rewrite, beginning with: <u>Sarah, whose</u>

Your new sentence will include:
   A. because she has lived
   B. because her father was
   C. she has lived in
   D. has lived in

20. Famous for its high academic standards, Harvard attracts the best and brightest students each year. Rewrite, beginning with: <u>Because of</u>

The next words will be:
   A. the best and the brightest
   B. its high academic standards
   C. attracting the best
   D. famous for its

21. *For the following ten questions, read the passage and then select the correct answer to the question. You may need to answer based on explicit information from the passage, as well as ideas that are suggested or implied in the passage.*

Our ability to measure brain activity is owing to the research of two European scientists. It was in 1929 that electrical activity in the human brain was first discovered. Hans Berger, the German psychiatrist who made the discovery, was despondent to find out, however, that many other scientists quickly dismissed his research. The work of Berger was confirmed three years later when Edgar Adrian, a Briton, clearly demonstrated that the brain, like the heart, is profuse in its electrical activity. Because of Adrian's work, we know that the electrical impulses in the brain, called brain waves, are a mixture of four different frequencies.

The purpose of the passage is to describe
   A. two opposing theories.
   B. important research about brain activity.
   C. a personal opinion about the work of two scientists.
   D. the different types of brain wave frequencies.

22. In the Black Hills, four visages protrude from the side of a mountain. The faces are those of four pivotal United States' presidents: George Washington, Thomas Jefferson, Theodore Roosevelt, and Abraham Lincoln. Washington was chosen on the basis of being the first president. Jefferson was instrumental in the writing of the American Declaration of Independence. Lincoln was selected on the basis of the mettle he demonstrated during the American Civil war, and Roosevelt for his development of Square Deal policy, as well as being a proponent of the construction of the Panama Canal.

From this passage, it seems reasonable to assume that these four presidents were chosen because
   A. of their outstanding courage.
   B. their faces would be aesthetically sympathetic to the natural surroundings.
   C. they helped to improve the national economy.
   D. their work was considered crucial to the progress of the nation.

23. The student readiness educational model is based on the view that students are individuals, each operating at different levels of ability. For some students, this might mean that they are operating above the average ability level of their contemporaries, while others may be functioning at a level that is below average. There are also students who are learning at the optimum learning level because they are being challenged and learning new things, but yet they do not feel overwhelmed or inundated by the new information. According to the student readiness approach, the onus falls on teachers to create classroom learning activities that will challenge the maximum number of students.

This passage is primarily about
   A. the rationale of one particular educational method.
   B. the individuality of various students.
   C. the burdens placed on teachers.
   D. the shortcomings of teachers and students.

24. Socio-economic status, rather than intellectual ability, may be the key to a child's success later in life. Consider two hypothetical elementary school students named John and Paul. Both of these children work hard, pay attention in the classroom, and are respectful to their teachers. Yet, Paul's father is a prosperous business tycoon, while John's has a menial job working in a factory. Despite the similarities in their academic aptitudes, the disparate economic situations of their parents means that Paul is nearly 30 times more likely than John to land a high-flying job by the time he reaches his fortieth year. In fact, John has only a 12% chance of finding and maintaining a job that would earn him even a median-level income.

We can conclude from information in this passage that
   A. academic ability is directly related to one's financial status later in life.
   B. children from high-income families are academically successful.
   C. children from affluent families are more likely to remain affluent as they grow older.
   D. most children from low-income families will get jobs in factories.

25. The most significant characteristic of any population is its age-sex structure, defined as the proportion of people of each gender in each different age group. The sex-age structure determines the potential for reproduction, and therefore population growth. Thus, the age-sex structure has social policy implications. For instance, a population with a high proportion of elderly citizens needs to consider its governmentally-funded pension schemes and health care systems carefully. Conversely, a greater percentage of young children in the population might imply that its educational funding and child welfare policies need to be evaluated. Accordingly, as the composition of a population changes over time, the government may need to re-evaluate its funding priorities.

Governmental funding decisions should primarily be based on
   A. the composition of the age and gender of its population.
   B. the number of elderly citizens in its population.
   C. the percentage of children in its population.
   D. social policy limitations.

36

26. Earthquakes occur when there is motion in the tectonic plates on the surface of the earth. The crust of the earth contains twelve such tectonic plates, which are from four to ten kilometers in length when located below the sea, although those on land can be from thirty to seventy kilometers long. Fault lines, the places where these plates meet, build up a great deal of pressure because the plates are constantly pressing on each other. Thus, the two plates will eventually shift or separate because the pressure on them is constantly increasing, and this build-up of energy needs to be released. When the plates shift or separate, we have the occurrence of an earthquake, also known as a seismic event.

The main purpose of the passage is
    A. to investigate a geological theory.
    B. to describe the events that result in a natural phenomenon.
    C. to propose a solution to a problem.
    D. to provide background to a personal observation.

27. The Hong Kong and Shanghai Bank Corporation (HSBC) skyscraper in Hong Kong is one of the world's most famous high-rise buildings. The building was designed so that it had many pre-built parts that were not constructed on site. This prefabrication made the project a truly international effort: the windows were manufactured in Austria, the exterior walls were fabricated in the United States, the toilets and air-conditioning were made in Japan, and many of the other components came from Germany.

The main idea of this passage is that
    A. prefabricated buildings are more international than those built in situ.
    B. countries should work together more often in construction projects.
    C. the HSBC building was an international project.
    D. the HSBC building is well-known because many countries were involved in its construction.

28. In December 406 A.D in what is now called Germany, 15,000 warriors crossed the frozen Rhine River and traveled into the Roman Empire of Gaul. A new historical epoch would soon be established in this former Roman Empire. Even though this period has diminished in historical significance in comparison to more recent events, the demise of the Roman Empire was certainly unprecedented in the fifth century. The six subsequent centuries that followed the collapse of the Roman Empire formed what we now call the Middle Ages.

According to the passage, the Roman Empire of Gaul
    A. was established during the middle ages.
    B. is now referred to as Germany.
    C. gradually collapsed throughout the Middle Ages.
    D. fell into ruin from 406 to 499 AD.

29. The study of philosophy usually deals with two key problem areas: human choice and human thought. A consideration of both of these problem areas includes scientific and artistic viewpoints on the nature of human life. The first problem area, human choice, asks whether human beings can really make decisions that can change their futures. It also investigates to what extent the individual's future is fixed and pre-determined by cosmic forces outside the control of human beings. In the second problem area, human thought, epistemology is considered. Epistemology means the study of knowledge; it should not be confused with ontology, the study of being or existence.

The primary purpose of the passage is
- A. to compare two areas of an academic discipline.
- B. to explain key aspects of a particular area of study.
- C. to contrast scientific and artistic views on a particular topic.
- D. to investigate two troublesome aspects of human behavior.

30. In 1859, some of Abraham Lincoln's associates began to put forward the idea that he should run for president of the United States, a notion that he discounted in his usual self-deprecating manner. Yet, as time passed, Lincoln began to write influential Republican Party leaders for their support. By 1860, Lincoln had garnered more public support, after having delivered public lectures and political speeches in various states. Despite being the underdog, Lincoln won 354 of the 466 total nominations at the Republican National Convention, and later, in November, 1860, the populace elected Lincoln as President of the United States.

This passage is mainly about
- A. the personal characteristics of Abraham Lincoln.
- B. the results of the 1860 US election.
- C. how Lincoln ran for and won the US presidency.
- D. how to be successful as a politician.

31. *For the following ten questions, you will see two sentences. Read the sentences, and then choose the best answer to the question.*

Owning a pet and taking care of it is a huge responsibility.

Taking care of a pet is like raising a child in many ways.

What does the second sentence do?
- A. It states the effect.
- B. It makes a comparison
- C. It gives an example.
- D. It offers a solution.

32. Everyone should take regular vacations in order maintain his or her physical health and well being.

Recent research demonstrates that taking a vacation helps to reduce the chances of getting certain diseases that are caused by high stress levels.

How are the two sentences related?
- A. They repeat the same idea.
- B. They give a problem and solution.
- C. They provide a general rule and a specific example.
- D. They create a contrast.

33. There has been an uproar among students on the university campus over the increase in student fees.

The university administration has stated that the fee increase was necessary because of inflation and increased operating costs.

What does the second sentence do?
    A. It presents a solution.
    B. It states a contradiction.
    C. It gives the effect.
    D. It provides explanation for a contentious topic.

34. The city has been struggling with increasing numbers of motorists attempting to park their cars in the downtown area.

The municipal government has introduced higher parking charges for those motorists wishing to park their cars downtown during peak times.

What does the second sentence do?
    A. It gives a solution to the problem that is stated in the first sentence.
    B. It explains the reason for the result mentioned in the first sentence.
    C. It exemplifies the first sentence.
    D. It draws a conclusion about what is stated in the first sentence.

35. Having good family relationships is essential in order to deal with the difficulties inherent in modern life.

Parents, siblings, and other relatives can help one cope, especially during times of hardship.

What does the second sentence do?
    A. It gives unexpected information.
    B. It provides an example for what is stated in the first sentence.
    C. It sums up the points raised in the first sentence.
    D. It reinforces the first sentence.

36. Global warming has led to the near demise of many types of wildlife.

The populations of many species have declined dramatically because of greenhouse gas emissions.

What does the second sentence do?
    A. It repeats the same idea as stated in the first sentence.
    B. It contradicts the evidence given in the first sentence.
    C. It presents a solution to the problem mentioned in the first sentence.
    D. It provides an application for the theory provided in the first sentence.

37. If not properly treated, high blood pressure negatively impacts upon the function of the heart and kidneys.

Many people live for years with untreated high blood pressure, and they experience no ill health as a result.

How are the two sentences related?
    A. They give a cause and an effect.
    B. They contradict each other.
    C. They repeat the same idea.
    D. The second analyzes the claim made in the first.

38. Rainy weather and lack of sunshine are believed to have negative effects on a person's mood.

There are higher numbers of suicides during prolonged periods of rain.

What does the second sentence do?
   A. It presents a solution to the problem mentioned in the first sentence.
   B. It contradicts the evidence given in the first sentence.
   C. It analyzes the claim made in first sentence.
   D. It sums up the points raised in the first sentence

39. People generally prefer modern architecture to more traditional types of building structures.

Many local residents have complained about the increasing amount of modern buildings in the city.

What does the second sentence do?
   A. It presents a solution to the problem mentioned in the first sentence.
   B. It gives unexpected information.
   C. It reinforces the claim made in first sentence.
   D. It provides an example for what is stated in the first sentence.

40. The school decided that chemistry class would no longer be a compulsory part of the curriculum.

The enrollment in chemistry class has fallen sharply since the class became voluntary.

What does the second sentence do?
   A. It explains the effect of the cause mentioned in the first sentence.
   B. It exemplifies the first sentence.
   C. It draws a conclusion about what is stated in the first sentence.
   D. It gives a solution to the problem that is stated in the first sentence.

41. *Solve the seventeen following arithmetic problems and select the correct answer from the choices given. You may use paper to work out your answers.*

$3.705 - 0.25 = ?$
   A. 3.455
   B. 3.68
   C. 3.5
   D. 3.55

42. $6.83 \times 5.2 = ?$
   A. 3.5516
   B. 35.526
   C. 35.516
   D. 355.16

43. 6/30 = ?
    A. .18
    B. .20
    C. .50
    D. .020

44. A job is shared by 4 workers, W, X, Y, and Z. Worker W does $^1/_4$ of the total hours. Worker X does $^1/_3$ of the total hours. Worker Y does $^1/_6$ of the total hours. What fraction represents the remaining hours allocated to person Z?
    A. $^2/_3$
    B. $^5/_{12}$
    C. $^1/_3$
    D. $^1/_4$

45. Which of the following is closest to 79.1 × 9.8 ?
    A. 790
    B. 800
    C. 7900
    D. 8000

46. Jenny's final grade for a course is based on the grades from two assignments, A and B. Assignment A counts toward 45% of her final grade. Assignment B counts toward 55% of her final grade. Which of the following equations is used to calculate her final grade for this course?
    A. .45A + .55B
    B. .55A + .45B
    C. 100(A + B)
    D. A + B

47. 48 is 40 percent of what number?
    A. 12
    B. 120
    C. 19.2
    D. 192

48. $4^1/_2 - 3^2/_5$ = ?
    A. $^1/_{10}$
    B. $^9/_{10}$
    C. $1^1/_{10}$
    D. $1^9/_{10}$

49. 0.16 ÷ .05 = ?
    A. .32
    B. 3.2
    C. 32
    D. .032

50. 1/16 = ?
    A. .0625%
    B. 6.25%
    C. 62.5%
    D. 625%

41

51. 3.13 + .004 + .071 = ?
     A. .388
     B. 3.88
     C. 3.205
     D. 3.844

52. Mary needs to get 750 signatures on a petition. Thus far, she has obtained 80% of the signatures she needs. How many more signatures does she still need?
     A. 50
     B. 150
     C. 300
     D. 600

53. 1/5 − 1/6 = ?
     A. 1/30
     B. −1/30
     C. 2/5
     D. 1/6

54. 99 ÷ 12 = ?
     A. .1212
     B. 12.12
     C. .825
     D. 8.25

55. The Johnson family is redecorating their home. They buy both wallpaper and paint. The wallpaper costs $12 per roll, and the paint costs $15 per bucket. They buy 3 buckets of paint. They also buy wallpaper. The total value of their purchase is $141. How many rolls of wallpaper did they buy?
     A. 7
     B. 8
     C. 15
     D. 16

56. Mrs. Brown owns an apple orchard. This year, her trees grew 1,300 apples. However, 25% of the apples were subsequently damaged as a result of adverse weather conditions. How many of Mrs. Brown's apples were damaged this year?
     A. 52
     B. 325
     C. 520
     D. 975

57. Which of the following is closest to $42^1/_4 \times 9^9/_{10}$?
     A. 420
     B. 430
     C. 42
     D. 43

58. *Solve the twelve following algebra problems and select the correct answer from the choices given. You may use paper to work out your answers.*

Simplify: $| 2 - 5 |$
   A. $(2 - 5)$
   B. $(-2 - 5)$
   C. 3
   D. -3

59. $125 = ?$
   A. $1.25 \div 10$
   B. $1.25 \div 10^2$
   C. 1.25×10
   D. 1.25×10^2

60. $\sqrt{2} = ?$
   A. 2
   B. $2^{1/2}$
   C. $2 \div 2$
   D. $2\sqrt{2}$

61. Which of the following sets of points $[(x_1, y_1); (x_2, y_2)]$ fall on the straight line represented by the following equation?

$y = x + 2$
   A. $(-2, -8); (2, 4)$
   B. $(-2, -4); (2, 8)$
   C. $(0, 2); (2, 4)$
   D. $(-2, -4); (2, 0)$

62. $(3x + 6y) + (2x - 4y) = ?$
   A. $x + 2y$
   B. $x - 2y$
   C. $5x + 2y$
   D. $5x - 2y$

63. $(4x^2 + 4x - 3) - (8x^2 - 6x + 6) = ?$
   A. $-4x^2 + 10x - 9$
   B. $-4x^2 + 10x + 9$
   C. $4x^2 + 10x + 9$
   D. $4x^2 + 10x - 9$

64. $(2x - 7)(x + 3) = ?$
   A. $2x^2 - x - 21$
   B. $2x^2 + x - 21$
   C. $2x^2 + x + 21$
   D. $2x^2 - x + 21$

43

65. $\sqrt{3} + 4\sqrt{3} = ?$

    A. $4\sqrt{3}^2$

    B. 12

    C. $\sqrt[4]{3}$

    D. $5\sqrt{3}$

66. $x^2 - x - 6 = ?$

    A. $(x - 2)(x - 3)$
    B. $(x - 2)(x + 3)$
    C. $(x + 2)(x + 3)$
    D. $(x + 2)(x - 3)$

67. $(-3 - -9) \div 2 = ?$

    A. -3
    B. 3
    C. -6
    D. 6

68. $\dfrac{5z - 5}{z} \div \dfrac{6z - 6}{5z^2} = ?$

    A. $\dfrac{6}{25z}$

    B. $\dfrac{30z^2 + 30}{5z^3}$

    C. $\dfrac{6z^2 - 6z}{25z^2 - 25z}$

    D. $\dfrac{25z}{6}$

69. What is the value of the expression $2x^3 - 2xy + 2y^2$ when $x = -2$ and $y = -2$?

    A. -32
    B. 32
    C. -16
    D. 16

70. *Solve the twenty following college-level math problems and select the correct answer from the choices given. You may use paper to work out your answers.*

$(x + 2) - (x^2 + x) = ?$
   A. $2x^2 + 2$
   B. $2x + 2 - x^2$
   C. $2x - 2 - x^2$
   D. $2 - x^2$

71. $\left(6y\right)^0 = ?$
   A. $6y$
   B. 6
   C. 1
   D. 0

72. $(-3x^2 + 12x + 4) - (x^2 - 4) = ?$
   A. $4x^2 + 12x$
   B. $-4x^2 + 12x + 8$
   C. $-4x^2 - 12x - 8$
   D. $-4x^2 + 12x - 8$

73. $12^4 \times 12^2 = ?$
   A. 24^6
   B. 12^2
   C. 12^6
   D. 12^8

74. $12xy - 8x^2y - 16y^2x^2 = ?$
   A. $4xy(3 + 2x - 4xy)$
   B. $4xy(3 - 2x + 4xy)$
   C. $4xy(3 + 2x + 4xy)$
   D. $4xy(3 - 2x - 4xy)$

75. If $x - 5 < 0$ and $y > x - 5$, then
   A. $y > 0$
   B. $y < 0$
   C. $y = 5$
   D. $y = -5$

76. If $c = \dfrac{a}{1-b}$, then $b = ?$

   A. c/a
   B. $a/c - 1$
   C. $-a/c + 1$
   D. $c - ca$

77. What number is next in the sequence?

    3, 9, 27, 81
- A. 99
- B. 108
- C. 162
- D. 243

78. Find the x and y intercepts of the following equation: $9x^2 + 4y^2 = 36$
- A. $(0, 2)$ and $(3, 0)$
- B. $(0, 4)$ and $(9, 0)$
- C. $(2, 0)$ and $(0, 3)$
- D. $(4, 0)$ and $(0, 9)$

79. Find the midpoint between the following coordinates: $(1, 2)$ and $(3, -4)$
- A. $(2, -1)$
- B. $(2, 1)$
- C. $(2, 3)$
- D. $(1.5, 0.5)$

80. $-|1 - 5| = ?$
- A. -4
- B. 4
- C. -6
- D. 6

81. $\sqrt{-16} = ?$
- A. $\sqrt{16}i$
- B. $4i$
- C. 4
- D. -4

82. $\sqrt{14x^5} \times \sqrt{6x^3} = ?$
- A. $\sqrt{20x^{15}}$
- B. $\sqrt{84x^{15}}$
- C. $2x^4\sqrt{21}$
- D. $2x^8\sqrt{21}$

83. What is the value of $\sum\limits_{x=1}^{3}\left(x^2 + 1\right)$
- A. 2
- B. 5
- C. 10
- D. 17

84. How many 2 letter combinations can be made from the letter set: B D F H J?
   A. 5
   B. 10
   C. 40
   D. 120

85. Which one of the following ordered pairs is a solution to the following system of equations?

$y = -3x - 2$
$y = x - 6$
   A. $(0, -2)$
   B. $(-2, -8)$
   C. $(-5, -11)$
   D. $(1, -5)$

86. $4 + 3(2\sqrt{x} - 3) = 25$, then $x =$
   A. $\sqrt{5}$
   B. 5
   C. 25
   D. 30

87. Find the area of the right triangle whose base is 3 and height is 4.
   A. $\sqrt{5}$
   B. 5
   C. 6
   D. 12

88. Consider the laws of sines and cosines. Sin $A^2 = ?$
   A. $1 - \cos A^2$
   B. $1 - \tan A^2$
   C. $\cos A^2$
   D. $\tan A^2$

89. Find the volume of a cone which has a radius of 6 and a height of 5.
   A. 30π
   B. 60π
   C. 120π
   D. 180π

ACCUPLACER PRACTICE TEST 2 – ANSWERS

1. The correct answer is C. This question is about the use of punctuation. "However, they were out of reach" is a complete sentence. It has a grammatical subject [they] and a verb [were]. "However" must be preceded by a period, and the new sentence must begin with a capital letter.

Compare the placement of "however" and the punctuation in these sentences: The child tried to grab the cookies from the shelf. They were, however, out of reach. When you use the word "however" in the middle of a sentence, "however" must be preceded by a comma and also followed by a comma.

2. The correct answer is C. "Covered in chocolate frosting" is a past participle phrase that describes the cake. In other words, the hostess is not covered in chocolate frosting. Therefore, the words "the cake" must follow the past participle phrase. Remember: past participle phrases are those that begin with verbs that end in -ed (in the case of regular verbs). You need to be sure that you have the participle phrase next to the noun that the phrase is describing.

3. The correct answer is A. This is another question about "parallelism." Be sure that all of the items you give in a list are of the same part of speech, nouns or verbs, for example. In other words, you should not use both nouns and verbs in a list. In addition, all of the verbs you use must be in the same tense. In answer A, both verbs are in the "to" form. The other answers combine -ing and -ed verbs.

4. The correct answer is A. The words "one which he could use to gaze at the stars" form a dependent relative clause. A relative clause often contains "that" or "which." A dependent clause cannot stand alone as a complete sentence. Since it is a non-restrictive (non-essential) relative clause, it must be preceded by a comma.

5. The correct answer is C. This question is another example of the inverted sentence structure. When a sentence begins with a negative phrase [no sooner, not only, never, etc.], the past perfect tense [had + past participle] must be used. In addition, the auxiliary verb "had" must be placed *in front of* the grammatical subject of the sentence [I].

6. The correct answer is B. This question tests your knowledge of conditional sentence structures. Conditional sentences often begin with the word *if*. Conditional sentences may express generalizations, as in this sentence. Therefore, the simple present tense (go) is used in the "If" clause, and the simple present (try) is also used in the main part of the sentence. The two parts of a conditional sentence must be separated by a comma.

7. The correct answer is B. Punctuation should be enclosed within the final quotation mark when giving dialogue. The word *said* shows that the comma needed.

8. The correct answer is D. The phrase "is known as" must be preceded with a noun phrase. "The experience of confusion about one's own identity" is a noun phrase. "Is known as" must not be preceded with a verb. No comma or pronoun (e.g., this, it) is needed.

9. The correct answer is C. "Upset from receiving the bad news" modifies or describes Mary. So this phrase must be followed with a comma. No additional commas are needed.

10. The correct answer is D. "Dilapidated and disheveled" is a past participle phrase that describes the house. Therefore, "Dilapidated and disheveled" must be followed by a comma.

11. The correct answer is B. The new sentence is: She was excited because she finally got that new car, which she had wanted for so long. We need to put a comma after "car" because "which" forms a non-restrictive relative clause. Remember that non-restrictive relative clauses convey non-essential information and that non-restrictive relative clauses must be preceded by a comma. The phrase "which she had wanted for so long" is non-essential because we have already identified the car earlier in the sentence with the phrase "that car."

12. The correct answer is C. The new sentence is: Unlike my physics tests, my math test will be easy to pass. The phrase "Unlike my physics test" is an adjectival phrase that modifies (or makes a comparison with) "my math test." Therefore, "my math test" must come directly after the comma.

13. The correct answer is D. The new sentence is: Having felt ill for days, she eventually came down with the flu. Phrases that begin with verbs in the -ing form are known as present participle phrases. In the new sentence, the present participle phrase "Having felt ill for days" modifies "she." Therefore, "she" must come directly after the comma.

14. The correct answer is A. The new sentence would be constructed as follows: She is not able to come to Hawaii with us because she cannot afford it. Remember that "because" is used to join subordinate clauses to sentences. Subordinate clauses contain a grammatical subject (she) and a verb (cannot afford), but they cannot stand alone as complete sentences.

15. The correct answer is C. The new sentence is: The game began after the referee blew his whistle. The word "after" begins the subordinate clause in the second part of the new sentence. Since the first part of the new sentence contains the past tense (began), the second part of the new sentence should also contain the past tense (blew). The words "the referee" form the grammatical subject of the subordinate clause.

16. The correct answer is B. The new sentence is: Whereas Thomas studied extensively for his final exams, Mary did not. The sentence begins with "whereas," a word which introduces a contrast or contradiction. Negative forms of the verb must be used in the second part of the sentence if the sentence begins with "whereas." So the negative form of the verb "did not" must be used in the second part of this sentence. Therefore, answers C and D are incorrect. Answer A is incorrect because "whereas" already conveys the idea of contrast, so "unlike" would repeat the idea of contrast.

17. The correct answer is D. The new sentence is: Unless he receives approval from his superiors, he will not get the promotion. Negative forms of the verb must be used in the second part of the sentence if the sentence begins with "unless." So the negative form of the verb "will not get" must be used in the second part of this sentence.

18. The correct answer is A. The new sentence would be constructed as follows: Although she gave her best effort, Barbara failed to complete the project on time. The word "although" is another subordinating conjunction used to join subordinate clauses to sentences.

19. The correct answer is D. The new sentence is: Sarah, whose father was a foreign diplomat, has lived in many locations around the world. The comma after "Sarah" indicates that a relative clause (e.g., whose) must be used. "Whose" is used to describe something that belongs to a person. In this sentence, we could say that Sarah's father "belongs" to her. So the word "father" must come after "whose." Remember that relative clauses include the following words: who, which, that, whom, whose.

20. The correct answer is B. The new sentence is: Because of its high academic standards, Harvard attracts the best and brightest students each year. The phrase linker "because of" is used to join a noun phrase to a sentence. Remember that noun phrases do not contain verbs and cannot stand alone as complete sentences. Answers A and D are adjectival phrases, and answer C contains a verb. Answer B is the only choice that contains a noun phrase.

21. The correct answer is B. For this type of question, you need to look carefully at the topic sentence: Our ability to measure brain activity is owing to the research of two European scientists. This sentence states that the passage is going to talk about brain research. We know that the research is important because the passage states: "Because of Adrian's work, we know that . . ."

22. The correct answer is D. The word "pivotal" in the passage means crucial to the progress of something.

49

23. The correct answer is A. Answer A is the most general answer. We also know that the paragraph is going to talk about the rationale (or reasons for something) because it begins with the phrase "is based on the view." The other answers provide specific information from the passage.

24. The correct answer is C. The passage states: "Paul is nearly 30 times more likely than John to land a high-flying job." High-flying means well-paid, so Paul will remain affluent. The other answer choices are incorrect interpretations of specific points from the passage.

25. The correct answer is A. This idea is contained in the topic sentence: The most significant characteristic of any population is its age-sex structure, defined as the proportion of people of each gender in each different age group. In the remainder of the passage, the author discusses how this idea relates to governmental funding. The other answers are too specific

26. The correct answer is B. The passage gives factual information about the events that cause an earthquake, which is a natural phenomenon. There is no investigation, proposal, or personal observation.

27. The correct answer is C. The passage states: "This prefabrication made the project a truly international effort." Ideas from answers A and B are not mentioned in the passage. The passage does not give the precise reason why the building is famous. It just states that the building is famous.

28. The correct answer is D. The passage states: "the demise of the Roman Empire was certainly unprecedented in the fifth century." We know that "demise" means ruin. We also know that the invasion took place in 406 AD, and that the fifth century ended in 499 AD.

29. The correct answer is B. The topic sentence states: "The study of philosophy usually deals with two key problem areas." The passage does not make any comparisons or contrasts, nor does it describe human behavior as "troublesome." It merely describes the key areas as "problem areas."

30. The correct answer is C. The main idea of the passage is to give information about how Lincoln became the president. Answers A and B are too specific, and answer D is an overgeneralization.

31. The correct answer is B. In the second sentence, the words "is like" indicate that a comparison is being made.

32. The correct answer is C. The first sentence makes a general statement about disease and health. The second sentence is more specific because it mentions "certain diseases."

33. The correct answer is D. The word "uproar" in the first sentence indicates that the topic is a contentious one. The word "because" in the second sentence indicates that an explanation is being given.

34. The correct answer is A. The problem is the increasing numbers of motorists trying to park. The solution is the higher parking charges. The higher parking charges are a solution because they are designed to discourage people from driving their cars and encourage them to take public transportation instead.

35. The correct answer is D. The words "is essential" show that a claim is being made in the first sentence. The word "hardship" in the second sentence also reinforces the idea of "difficulties" in the first sentence.

36. The correct answer is A. The words "near demise" in the first sentence have the same meaning as "declined dramatically" in the second sentence. Global warming is a fact, not a theory.

37. The correct answer is B. The words "negatively impacts" in the first sentence contradict the words "experience no ill health" in the second sentence.

38. The correct answer is C. The words "are believed to have" in the first sentence indicate that a claim is being made. The second sentence is suggesting that people take their own lives because of low mood due to poor weather.

39. The correct answer is B. If people really prefer modern architecture, then we would not expect them to complain about the modern buildings. Therefore, the second sentence gives unexpected information.

40. The correct answer is A. The word "since" in the second sentence indicates that a reason is being given.

41. The correct answer is A. When you add on your scratch paper, be sure to line all of the decimals up in a column like this:

$$\begin{array}{r} 3.705 \\ -\,0.250 \\ \hline 3.455 \end{array}$$

Remember to add zeros where necessary at the beginning or end of the numbers in order to make the decimal points line up.

42. The correct answer is C. Be careful with the decimal point positions when you do long multiplication.

$$\begin{array}{r} 6.83 \\ \times\quad 5.2 \\ \hline 1.366 \\ 34.150 \\ \hline 35.516 \end{array}$$

43. The correct answer is B. You will need to do long division to determine the answer:

$$\begin{array}{r} .20 \\ 30)\overline{6.00} \\ \underline{6.00} \\ 0 \end{array}$$

44. The correct answer is D. The sum of the work from all four people must be equal to 100%, simplified to 1. In other words, they make up the total hours by working together:

W + X + Y + Z = 1

1/4 + 1/3 + 1/6 + Z = 1

Now, find the lowest common denominator of the fractions:

1/4 + 1/3 + 1/6 + Z = 1

3 x 4 = 12 and 2 x 6 = 12. So the lowest common denominator is 12.

Now convert the fractions:

1/4 x 3/3 = 3/12
1/3 x 4/4 = 4/12
1/6 x 2/2 = 2/12

Now add the fractions together:

3/12 + 4/12 + 2/12 + Z = 1
9/12 + Z = 1

9/12 − 9/12 + Z = 1 − 9/12
Z = 1 − 3/4
Z = 1/4

45. The correct answer is A. For estimation problems like this, round the decimals up or down to the nearest whole number. 79.1 is rounded down to 79, and 9.8 is rounded up to 10. Then do long multiplication:

$$\begin{array}{r} 79 \\ \times\ 10 \\ \hline 790 \end{array}$$

46. The correct answer is A. The two assignments are being given different percentages, so each assignment needs to have its own variable:

A for assignment A
B for assignment B

So the value of assignment A is .45A and the value of assignment B is .55B

The final grade is the sum of the values of these two variables: .45A + .55B

47. The correct answer is B. 40 percent is equal to 0.40. The phrase "of what number" indicates that we need to divide the two amounts given in the problem:

48 ÷ 0.40 = 120.

We can check this result as follows: 120 × 0.40 = 48

48. The correct answer is C. Questions like this test your knowledge of mixed numbers. Mixed numbers are those that contain a whole number and a fraction. If the fraction on the first mixed number is greater than the fraction on the second mixed number, you can subtract the whole numbers and the fractions separately. Remember to use the lowest common denominator on the fractions.

$4 - 3 = 1$

$1/2 - 2/5 =$
$5/10 - 4/10 =$
$1/10$

Therefore, the result is $1^1/_{10}$

49. The correct answer is B. You must do long division until you have no remainder:

```
        3.2
.05) .16
      .15
       10
       10
        0
```

50. The correct answer is B.

$1 \div 16 = 0.0625$
$0.0625 = 6.25\%$

51. The correct answer is C. When you add on your scratch paper, be sure to line all of the decimals up in a column like this, adding zeros where necessary at the beginning or end of the numbers in order to make the decimal points line up:

```
3.130
0.004
0.071
3.205
```

52. The correct answer is B. We know that Mary has already gotten 80% of the signatures. However, the question is asking how many signatures she still needs.

So, $100\% - 80\% = 20\%$
$20\% = .20$

Now do the multiplication:

$750 \times .20 = 150$

53. The correct answer is A. In fraction problems like this, you have to find the lowest common denominator. [The denominator is the number on the bottom of the fraction.] In other words, before you subtract the fractions, you have to change them so that the bottom numbers for each fraction are the same, which in this case is thirtieths. You do this by multiplying the numerator [top number] by the same number you use on the denominator for each fraction.

$1/5 \times 6/6 = 6/30$
$1/6 \times 5/5 = 5/30$

When you have got both fractions in the same denominator, you subtract them:

6/30 − 5/30 = 1/30

54. The correct answer is D. You must do long division until you have no remainder.

$$
\begin{array}{r}
8.25 \\
12\overline{)99} \\
\underline{96} \\
30 \\
\underline{24} \\
60 \\
\underline{60} \\
0
\end{array}
$$

55. The correct answer is B. If each item has a different price, you must assign a different variable to each item. So, let's say that the number of buckets of paint is P and the number of rolls of wallpaper is W. Now let's make an equation to express the above problem:

$(P \times \$15) + (W \times \$12) = \$141$

We know that the number of buckets of paint is 3, so let's put that in the equation and solve it:

$(P \times \$3) + (W \times \$12) = \$141$
$(3 \times \$15) + (W \times \$12) = \$141$
$\$45 + (W \times \$12) = \$141$
$\$45 - \$45 + (W \times \$12) = \$141 - \$45$
$\$0 + (W \times \$12) = \$96$
$\$12W = \$96$
$\$12W \div \$12 = \$96 \div \$12$
$W = 8$

56. The correct answer is B.

25% = .25
1300 x .25 = 325

57. The correct answer is A. For estimation problems like this, round the fractions up or down to the nearest whole number. Then do the multiplication:

42 x 10 = 420

58. The correct answer is C. Remember that when you see numbers between lines like this $|-2|$, you are being asked the absolute value. Absolute value is always a positive number. So for this question:

$|2 - 5| = |-3|$
$|-3| = 3$

59. The correct answer is D. For questions like this, look at the answer choices and decide which ones might be feasible. Using common sense, we can see that the division problems will result in too small a number. Then do the math on the remaining answer choices:

$1.25 \times 10 = 12.5$
$1.25 \times 10^2 = 1.25 \times 100 = 125$

60. The correct answer is B. This question is testing your knowledge of exponent laws. Remember that

$$\sqrt{x} = x^{1/2}$$

61. The correct answer is C. To solve problems like this one, begin by substituting 0 for x.

$y = x + 2$
$y = 0 + 2$
$y = 2$

Therefore, the coordinates (0, 2) solve the problem.

Now check the other coordinates:

$y = x + 2$
$y = 2 + 2$
$y = 4$

So (2, 4) is also correct.

62. The correct answer is C. First perform the operations on the parentheses:

$(3x + 6y) + (2x - 4y) =$
$3x + 6y + 2x - 4y$

Then place the x and y terms together:

$3x + 2x + 6y - 4y$

Finally add or subtract the x and y terms:

$3x + 2x + 6y - 4y =$
$5x + 2y$

63. The correct answer is A. First perform the operations on the parentheses. Remember that two negatives make a positive:

$(4x^2 + 4x - 3) - (8x^2 - 6x + 6) =$
$4x^2 + 4x - 3 - 8x^2 + 6x - 6$

Then place the x and y terms together:

$4x^2 + 4x - 3 - 8x^2 + 6x - 6 =$
$4x^2 - 8x^2 + 4x + 6x - 3 - 6$

Finally add or subtract the x and y terms:

$4x^2 - 8x^2 + 4x + 6x - 3 - 6 =$
$-4x^2 + 10x - 9$

64. The correct answer is A. Remember to use the F-O-I-L method when you multiply:

FIRST: $2x \times x = 2x^2$
OUTSIDE: $2x \times 3 = 6x$
INSIDE: $-7 \times x = -7x$
LAST: $-7 \times 3 = -21$

Then add all of the above once you have completed F-O-I-L:

$2x^2 + 6x + -7x + -21 =$
$2x^2 + 6x - 7x - 21 =$
$2x^2 - x - 21$

65. The correct answer is D. Add the numbers in front of the square root signs.

$$\sqrt{3} + 4\sqrt{3} = 1\sqrt{3} + 4\sqrt{3} = 5\sqrt{3}$$

66. The correct answer is D. If you notice that the answer choices are all the same, except for the + or − signs, you may just want to try to multiply the answer choices to see which answer agrees to the equation given in the question:

(A) $(x - 2)(x - 3) = x^2 - 5x + 6$
(B) $(x - 2)(x + 3) = x^2 + x - 6$
(C) $(x + 2)(x + 3) = x^2 + 5x + 6$
(D) $(x + 2)(x - 3) = x^2 - x - 6$

67. The correct answer is B. Perform the operations on the parentheses first:

$(-3 - -9) \div 2 =$
$(-3 + 9) \div 2 =$
$6 \div 2$

Then divide: $6 \div 2 = 3$

68. The correct answer is D. When dividing fractions, you need to invert the second fraction and then multiply the two fractions together.

$$\frac{5z - 5}{z} \div \frac{6z - 6}{5z^2} =$$
$$\frac{5z - 5}{z} \times \frac{5z^2}{6z - 6}$$

When multiplying fractions, you multiply the numerator of the first fraction by the numerator of the second fraction and denominator of the first fraction by the denominator of the second fraction.

$$\frac{5z-5}{z} \times \frac{5z^2}{6z-6} =$$

$$\frac{25z^3 - 25z^2}{6z^2 - 6z}$$

Then look at the numerator and denominator from the result of the previous step to see if you can factor and simplify. In this case, the numerator and denominator have the common factor of $(z^2 - z)$.

$$\frac{25z^3 - 25z^2}{6z^2 - 6z} =$$

$$\frac{25z(z^2 - z)}{6(z^2 - z)} =$$

$$\frac{25z}{6}$$

69. The correct answer is C. To solve this problem, put in the values for x and y and multiply. Remember to be careful when multiplying negative numbers:

$2x^3 - 2xy + 2y^2 =$
$(2 \times -2^3) - (2 \times -2 \times -2) + 2(-2 \times -2) =$
$(2 \times -8) - (2 \times 4) + (2 \times 4) =$
$-16 - 8 + 8 =$
-16

70. The correct answer is D. Perform the operations on the parentheses first:

$(x + 2) - (x^2 + x) =$
$x + 2 - x^2 - x$

Then put the x terms together:

$x - x + 2 - x^2 =$
$2 - x^2$

71. The correct answer is C. Any number to the power of zero is equal to 1.

72. The correct answer is B. Perform the operations on the parentheses first:

$(-3x^2 + 12x + 4) - (x^2 - 4) =$
$-3x^2 + 12x + 4 - x^2 + 4$

Then group the x^2 terms together:

$$-3x^2 + 12x + 4 - x^2 + 4 =$$
$$-3x^2 - x^2 + 12x + 4 + 4 =$$
$$-4x^2 + 12x + 8$$

73. The correct answer is C. Remember that if the base number is the same, and the problem asks you to multiply, you simply add the exponents:

$$12^4 \times 12^2 = 12^{4+2} = 12^6$$

74. The correct answer is D. In order to factor an equation, you first have to figure out what variables are common to each term of the equation. Let's look at this equation: $12xy - 8x^2y - 16y^2x^2$

Factor out xy: $12xy - 8x^2y - 16y^2x^2 = xy(12 - 8x - 16yx)$

Then, think about integers. We can see that all of the terms inside the parentheses are divisible by 4. Now let's factor out the 4. In order to do this, we divide each term inside the parentheses by 4:

$$xy(12 - 8x - 16yx) =$$
$$4xy(3 - 2x - 4yx) =$$
$$4xy(3 - 2x - 4xy)$$

75. The correct answer is A. For inequality problems, you should first solve the equation for x:

$$x - 5 < 0 =$$
$$x - 5 + 5 < 0 + 5 =$$
$$x < 5$$

Now solve for y by replacing x with its value:

$$y > x - 5 =$$
$$y > 5 - 5 =$$
$$y > 0$$

76. The correct answer is C. First you need to get rid of the fraction. To eliminate the fraction, multiply each side of the equation by the denominator of the fraction.

$$c = \frac{a}{1-b}$$

$$c \times (1 - b) = \frac{a}{1-b} \times (1 - b)$$

$$c \times (1 - b) = a$$

Then simplify the side of the equation with the variable that you need to isolate, in this case b.

$$c \times (1 - b) = a$$

$$c(1-b) \div c = a \div c$$

$$1 - b = \frac{a}{c}$$

Then isolate b by dealing with the integer and the negative sign in order to solve the problem.

$$1 - b = \frac{a}{c}$$
$$1 - 1 - b = \frac{a}{c} - 1$$
$$-b = \frac{a}{c} - 1$$
$$-b \times -1 = \left(\frac{a}{c} - 1\right) \times -1$$
$$b = -\frac{a}{c} + 1$$

77. The correct answer is D. To solve this kind of problem, you need to find the relationship between each of the numbers given. If we look carefully at the numbers given above, we can see that:

$3 \times 3 = 9$
$9 \times 3 = 27$
$27 \times 3 = 81$

Therefore, we have to multiply 81 by 3 to find the solution: $81 \times 3 = 243$

78. The correct answer is C. For questions about x and y intercepts, substitute 0 for x and y to solve the problem. First look at the solution for the x intercept:

$9x^2 + 4y^2 = 36$
$9x^2 + (4 \times 0) = 36$
$9x^2 + 0 = 36$
$9x^2 \div 9 = 36 \div 9$
$x^2 = 4$
$x = 2$

So the x intercept is (2, 0)

Here is the solution for y intercept:

$9x^2 + 4y^2 = 36$
$(9 \times 0) + 4y^2 = 36$
$0 + 4y^2 = 36$
$4y^2 \div 4 = 36 \div 4$
$y^2 = 9$
$y = 3$

So the y intercept is (0, 3)

79. The correct answer is A. This question covers coordinate geometry. Remember that in order to find midpoints on a line, you need to use the midpoint formula. For two points on a graph (x_1, y_1) and (x_2, y_2), the midpoint is: $(x_1 + x_2) \div 2$, $(y_1 + y_2) \div 2$

Now calculate for x and y:

$(1 + 3) \div 2 = $ midpoint x, $(2 + -4) \div 2 = $ midpoint y
$4 \div 2 = $ midpoint x, $-2 \div 2 = $ midpoint y
$2 = $ midpoint x, $-1 = $ midpoint y

80. The correct answer is A. Remember that the absolute value is always a positive number.

$-|1 - 5| =$
$-|-4|$

So the absolute value of -4 is 4. However, notice the negative sign in front of the absolute value symbol. Therefore, you have to give the negative of the absolute value for your final result.

$-|-4| = -(4) = -4$

81. The correct answer is B. Note that it is not possible to find the square root of a negative number by using real numbers. Therefore, you will have to use imaginary numbers to solve this problem. Imaginary numbers are represented by the variable i.

So first determine what the square root of the number would be if the number were positive: $\sqrt{16} = 4$

Now multiply that result by i: $4 \times i = 4i$

82. The correct answer is C. First do the multiplication. When there are exponents inside the square root signs, you add them together to get your product.

$$\sqrt{14x^5} \times \sqrt{6x^3} = \sqrt{84x^8}$$

Then factor the integer inside the square root sign and simplify.

$$\sqrt{84x^8} =$$
$$\sqrt{4 \times 21x^8} =$$
$$2\sqrt{21x^8}$$

Finally, remember that the square root of any number is that number to the ½ power.

For example, $\sqrt{x} = x^{\frac{1}{2}}$

$$2\sqrt{21x^8} =$$
$$2 \times \sqrt{21} \times x^{\frac{8}{2}} =$$

$$2 \times \sqrt{21} \times x^4 =$$
$$2x^4 \sqrt{21}$$

83. The correct answer is D. If $x = 1$ and the value above the sigma sign is 3, you need to find the individual products for $x^2 + 1$ for $x = 1$, $x = 2$, and $x = 3$.

For $x = 1$, $x^2 + 1 = 2$
For $x = 2$, $x^2 + 1 = 5$
For $x = 3$, $x^2 + 1 = 10$

Then you add these three products together to get your result.

$2 + 5 + 10 = 17$

84. The correct answer is B. For this type of question, be sure to notice if you are being asked to calculate permutations or combinations because the formulas are different. To determine the number of combinations of S at a time that can be made from a set containing N items, you need this formula:

$(N!) \div [(N - S)! \times S!]$

In the problem above, $S = 2$ and $N = 5$ (because there are five letters in the set).

Now substitute the values for S and N:

$(5 \times 4 \times 3 \times 2 \times 1) \div [(5 - 2)! \times (2!)] = (5 \times 4 \times 3 \times 2) \div [(3 \times 2 \times 1) \times (2 \times 1)] = 120 \div 12 = 10$

85. The correct answer is D. First, subtract the equations:

$$y = -3x - 2$$
$$\underline{-(y = x - 6)}$$
$$0 = -4x + 4$$
$$1 = x$$

Then plug in the values for x:

If $x = 1$, then for $y = -3x - 2$
$y = (-3 \times 1) - 2$
$y = -5$

For the second equation:

$y = x - 6$
$y = 1 - 6$
$y = -5$

86. The correct answer is C. In equations that have both integers and square roots, deal with the integers that are outside the parentheses first:

$$4 + 3(2\sqrt{x} - 3) = 25$$
$$4 - 4 + 3(2\sqrt{x} - 3) = 25 - 4$$
$$3(2\sqrt{x} - 3) = 21$$

Then carry out the operations for the parenthetical terms:

$$3(2\sqrt{x} - 3) = 21$$
$$6\sqrt{x} - 9 = 21$$
$$6\sqrt{x} - 9 + 9 = 21 + 9$$
$$6\sqrt{x} = 30$$
$$6\sqrt{x} \div 6 = 30 \div 6$$
$$\sqrt{x} = 5$$

5 is the square root of 25.

87. The correct answer is C. To solve this problem, you need the following equation:

Triangle area = (base × height) ÷ 2

Now substitute the amounts for base and height:

area = (3 × 4) ÷ 2 = 12 ÷ 2 = 6

88. The correct answer is A. Sin A^2 is always equal to 1 − cos A^2.

89. The correct answer is B. To find the volume of a cone, you need this formula:

Cone volume = (π × radius^2 × height) ÷ 3

Now substitute the values for base and height:

volume = ($\pi 6^2$ × 5) ÷ 3
($\pi 36$ × 5) ÷ 3
$\pi 180$ ÷ 3
60π

ACCUPLACER PRACTICE TEST 3

1. *Select the best substitute for the underlined parts of the following ten sentences. The first answer [choice A] is identical to the original sentence. If you think the original sentence is best, then choose A as your answer.*

   While at the mall, <u>a paperback book was purchased by me.</u>
   - A. a paperback book was purchased by me.
   - B. the paperback book was purchased by me.
   - C. a paperback book's purchase was made by me.
   - D. I purchased a paperback book.

2. <u>We just arrived</u> at the airport when Tom's flight landed.
   - A. We just arrived
   - B. Just had we arrived
   - C. We had just arrived
   - D. Just we were arriving

3. We were going to go away on <u>vacation. And then</u> our plans changed.
   - A. Vacation. And then
   - B. vacation, then
   - C. vacation and then
   - D. vacation, and then

4. John's favorite hobbies are <u>to read and to swim.</u>
   - A. to read and to swim.
   - B. to read and swimming.
   - C. reading and swimming.
   - D. reading and to swim.

5. <u>Exasperated, Bill finally lost his temper</u> with his unruly children.
   - A. Exasperated, Bill finally lost his temper
   - B. Bill was exasperated, finally lost his temper
   - C. Bill, was exasperated, finally lost his temper
   - D. Exasperating Bill, finally lost

6. He was planning on finding a new <u>apartment that</u> would accommodate all of his oversized furniture.
   - A. apartment that
   - B. apartment. One that
   - C. apartment, that
   - D. apartment so that

7. "I can't believe you won the <u>lottery", Sarah</u> exclaimed.
   - A. lottery", Sarah
   - B. lottery." Sarah
   - C. lottery!" Sarah
   - D. lottery" Sarah

8. <u>In spite of he studied hard, he</u> failed the exam.
    A. In spite of he studied hard, he
    B. In spite of studying hard, he
    C. In spite of he studying hard, he
    D. In spite of studied hard, he

9. Jane is the <u>taller of</u> her four sisters.
    A. taller of
    B. taller than
    C. most tall of
    D. tallest of

10. <u>If stealing money from your employer,</u> you could be charged with the crime of embezzlement.
    A. If stealing money from your employer,
    B. Stealing money from your employer
    C. If you steal money from your employer,
    D. If you steal money from your employer

11. *Rewrite the following ten sentences mentally in your own head. Follow the directions given for the formation of the new sentence. Remember that your new sentence should be grammatically correct and convey the same meaning as the original sentence.*

After checking the extent of the man's injuries, the paramedics put him into the ambulance. Rewrite, beginning with: <u>Once they</u>

The next words will be:
    A. were checking
    B. had checked
    C. had been checking
    D. will check

12. The professor's praise of my exam score in front of the other students embarrassed me. Rewrite, beginning with: <u>I was embarrassed when</u>

The next words will be:
    A. the professor praised
    B. the professor praising
    C. the professor, praising
    D. the professor, he praised

13. Both Minnesota and Wisconsin get extremely cold in the winter. Rewrite, beginning with: <u>Like Minnesota,</u>

The next words will be:
    A. Wisconsin gets
    B. and Wisconsin
    C. extreme cold
    D. it is

14. Rich in natural beauty and abundant in wildlife, the Grand Canyon is a popular tourist destination. Rewrite, beginning with: <u>The Grand Canyon</u>

Your new sentence will include:
   A. because being
   B. because it being
   C. because it is
   D. because being it

15. My sister was ill with the flu, so she stayed home from school.

Rewrite, beginning with: <u>My sister,</u>

The next words will be:
   A. ill and
   B. she was ill
   C. was ill
   D. who was ill

16. If it rains tomorrow, we will have to cancel the picnic. Rewrite, beginning with: <u>In the event of</u>

The next words will be:
   A. raining
   B. rains
   C. rain
   D. it rains

17. The team lost the championship game, and the players were so disappointed. Rewrite, beginning with: <u>The team was</u>

Your new sentence will include:
   A. although it lost
   B. when it lost
   C. and it lost
   D. because the loss of

18. Despite years of training, he was not selected for the Olympics. Rewrite, beginning with: <u>Although</u>

The next words will be:
   A. he trained for years
   B. training for years
   C. years of training
   D. years he trained

65

19. As he watched television, he fell asleep and began snoring. Rewrite, beginning with: <u>Watching</u>

   The next words will be:
   - A. television he fell
   - B. and fell
   - C. television, he fell
   - D. television, and falling

20. Many international students suffer from homesickness during their studies in the United States. Rewrite, beginning with: <u>Suffering from</u>

   Your new sentence will include:
   - A. common international student's
   - B. is common studying
   - C. is commonality of international students
   - D. is common among international students

21. *For the following ten questions, read the passage and then select the correct answer to the question. You may need to answer based on explicit information from the passage, as well as ideas that are suggested or implied in the passage.*

   American Major League Baseball consisted of only a handful of teams when the National League was founded in 1876. Yet, baseball has grown in popularity by leaps and bounds over the years, resulting in increased ticket sales for games and bolstering the profits of its investors. The increased demand from the public, in turn, precipitated the formation of a new division, known as the American League, in 1901. Additionally, new teams are formed from time to time in accordance with regional demand, such as the Colorado Rockies in Denver, Colorado, and the Devil Rays in Tampa Bay, Florida.

   The main purpose of the passage is:
   - A. To give examples of two popular American baseball teams.
   - B. To provide specific information about the process of forming new baseball teams.
   - C. To trace historical developments relating to the popularity of baseball.
   - D. To criticize Americans who depend on baseball for entertainment.

22. The use of computers in the stock market helps to control national and international finance. These controls were originally designed in order to create long-term monetary stability and protect shareholders from catastrophic losses. Yet, the high level of automation now involved in buying and selling shares means that computer-to-computer trading could result in a downturn in the stock market. Such a slump in the market, if not properly regulated, could bring about a computer-led stock market crash. For this reason, regulations have been put in place by NASDAQ, AMEX, and FTSE.

   From this passage, one could infer that:
   - A. Regulations on computer-to-computer trading are considered to be a financial necessity.
   - B. There are negative public views about regulations on computer-to-computer trading.
   - C. NASDAQ, AMEX, and FTSE were initially opposed to establishing regulations on computer-to-computer trading.
   - D. The role of computers in international markets has not been modified over time.

23. Airline travel is generally considered to be an extremely safe mode of transportation. Statistics reveal that far fewer individuals are killed each year in airline accidents than in crashes involving automobiles. In spite of this safety record, airlines deploy ever-increasingly strict standards governing the investigation of aircraft crashes. Information gleaned from the investigation of aircraft crashes is utilized in order to prevent such tragedies from occurring again in the future.

The main purpose of this passage is:
   A. To contrast automotive travel with airline travel.
   B. To compare statistics on deaths related to transportation accidents.
   C. To explain the reasons for the investigation of aircraft crashes.
   D. To justify government spending on aircraft accident investigations.

24. In 1749, British surveyors spotted a high peak in the distant range of the Himalayas. More than 100 years later, in 1852, another survey was completed, which confirmed that this peak was the highest mountain in the world. Later named Mount Everest, this peak was considered to be the world's highest mountain until 1986. At that time, George Wallerstein from the University of Washington posited that another Himalayan mountain, named K-2, was higher than Everest. It took an expedition of Italian scientists, who used a surfeit of technological devices, to disprove Wallerstein's claim.

According to the passage, which one of the following statements is correct?
   A. Since 1749, Mount Everest has universally been considered to be the tallest mountain in the world.
   B. Wallerstein fell into disrepute in the academic community after his claims were disproved.
   C. The Italian team confirmed that Everest was, in fact, the tallest mountain in the world.
   D. In spite of a lack of technologically-advanced equipment, Italian scientists were able to refute Wallerstein's hypothesis.

25. Clones have been used for centuries in the field of horticulture. For instance, florists have traditionally made clones of geraniums and other plants by taking cuttings and re-planting them in fresh soil. Despite the predictability of cloning in the realm of plants and flowers, however, cloning has arguably taken on sinister undertones, thanks to the rapid development of science and technology. Some fear the ethical ramifications that will inevitably occur if cloning is extended to the human species.

We can conclude from the information in this passage that:
   A. Cloning is a somewhat controversial subject.
   B. Cloning has fallen out of favor with horticulturalists.
   C. In spite of certain misgivings, many people support human cloning.
   D. Technological advances have impeded the use of cloning.

26. Owing to the powerful and destructive nature of tornadoes, there are, perhaps not surprisingly, a number of myths and misconceptions surrounding them. For instance, many people mistakenly believe that tornadoes never occur over rivers, lakes, and oceans; yet, waterspouts, tornadoes that form over bodies of water, often move onshore and cause extensive damage to coastal areas. In addition, tornadoes can accompany hurricanes and tropical storms as they move to land. Another common myth about tornadoes is that damage to built structures, like houses and office buildings, can be avoided if windows are opened prior to the impact of the storm.

What can be inferred about the public's knowledge of tornadoes?
   A. A large number of people know how to avoid tornado damage.
   B. Most people appreciate the risk of death associated with tornadoes.
   C. Some members of the public know how to regulate the pressure inside buildings.
   D. Many people are not fully aware of certain key information about tornadoes.

27. Born in France in 1896, Jean Piaget was one of the most influential thinkers in the area of child development in the twentieth century. Piaget posited that children go through a stage of assimilation as they grow to maturity. Assimilation refers to the process of transforming one's environment in order to bring about its conformance to innate cognitive schemes and structures. Schemes used in infant breast feeding and bottle feeding are examples of assimilation because the child utilizes his or her innate capacity for sucking to complete both tasks.

Why does the writer mention bottle feeding in the above paragraph?
   A. To identify one of the important features of assimilation.
   B. To exemplify the assimilation process.
   C. To describe the importance of assimilation.
   D. To explain difficulties children face during assimilation.

28. Inherent social and cultural biases pervaded the manner in which archeological findings were investigated during the early nineteenth century because little attention was paid to the roles that wealth, status, and nationality played in the recovery and interpretation of artifacts. However, in the 1860s Charles Darwin established the theory that human beings are the ultimate product of a long biological evolutionary process. Darwinian theory infiltrated the discipline of archeology and heavily influenced the manner in which archeological artifacts were recovered and analyzed. As a result of Darwinism, there was a surge in artifacts excavated from African and Asian localities by the late 1900s.

Based on the information above, what can be inferred about the early 1900s?
   A. There were few archeological findings from Africa and Asia.
   B. Darwinian theory had little effect on archeology.
   C. All archeological findings were culturally biased in the early 1900s.
   D. Charles Darwin was responsible for the recovery of many artifacts.

29. The tradition of music in the western world originated in the genre of chanting. Chant, a monophonic form of music, was the dominant mode of music prior to the thirteenth century. The semantic origins of the word "monophonic" are of special interest. "Mono" is from a Greek word which means one thing alone or by itself. "Phonic" is also Greek in origin, and it means sound. Accordingly, monophonic music consists of only one sound or voice that combines various notes in a series.

What is the main idea of this passage?
   A. The origins of music in the western world.
   B. The history of music during two previous centuries.
   C. The semantics of a particular Greek word.
   D. The variety of symphonic forms.

30. Various health risks are posed by processed or convenience food. Packaged food often contains chemicals, such as additives to enhance the color of the food or preservatives that give the food a longer life. Food additives are detrimental to the health for a number of reasons. First of all, they are not natural and may perhaps be linked to disease in the long term. In addition, they may block the body's ability to absorb energy and nutrients from food, such as essential vitamins and minerals that are required for healthy bodily function.

How does the passage support its claim about food additives?
   A. By explaining their purpose.
   B. By giving reasons for their dangers.
   C. By discussing specific medical case studies.
   D. By linking them to preservatives.

31. *For the following ten questions, you will see two sentences. Read the sentences, and then choose the best answer to the question.*

Tourists face many problems caused by miscommunication when they travel abroad.

Increasing numbers of tourists have been travelling overseas in recent years.

How are the two sentences related?
   A. They repeat the same idea.
   B. They give a problem and solution.
   C. They provide a general rule and a specific example.
   D. They create a contrast.

32. The hurricane devastated the coastal area.

Many residents are now homeless.

What does the second sentence do?
   A. It states the effect.
   B. It gives an example.
   C. It offers a solution.
   D. It makes a comparison.

33. It is important to get along well with one's neighbors in a local community.

Many people prefer to live insular lives, and they experience no negative consequences from being isolated from their fellow citizens.

How are the two sentences related?
   A. They present problems and solutions.
   B. They contradict one another.
   C. They give a cause and its effect.
   D. They provide explanations for a contentious topic.

34. Increasing levels of pollution have an extremely adverse effect on the environment.

The government has established regulations to limit the amount of noxious fumes emitted into the atmosphere.

What does the second sentence do?
   A. It exemplifies the first sentence.
   B. It explains the reason for the result mentioned in the first sentence.
   C. It gives a solution to the problem that is stated in the first sentence.
   D. It draws a conclusion about what is stated in the first sentence.

35. Voting at national and state elections is an important duty of every citizen.

Statistics reveal that voter turnout at the last election had fallen by 38 percent.

What does the second sentence do?
   A. It reinforces the claim made in first sentence.
   B. It sums up the points raised in the first sentence.
   C. It provides an example for what is stated in the first sentence.
   D. It gives unexpected information.

36. Certain psychologists believe that children of divorced parents often do poorly at school.

Students from so-called "broken homes" are prone to problems with their academic performance.

What does the second sentence do?
   A. It repeats the same idea as stated in the first sentence.
   B. It contradicts the evidence given in the first sentence.
   C. It provides an application for the theory provided in the first sentence.
   D. It presents a solution to the problem mentioned in the first sentence.

37. Existing inhabitants experienced great distress and hardship when their lands were invaded and colonized.

Colonizers from nations such as Great Britain and Spain brought many diseases to foreign lands, which ultimately killed the native dwellers.

What does the second sentence do?
  A. It sums up the points raised in the first sentence.
  B. It presents a solution to the problem mentioned in the first sentence.
  C. It provides a specific example for the general claim made in the first sentence.
  D. It repeats the same idea as stated in the first sentence.

38. Most universities have heavy penalties for academic dishonesty and cheating.

Some students buy their essays online, rather than preparing the work themselves.

How are the two sentences related?
  A. They contradict each other.
  B. They provide a contrast.
  C. They repeat the same idea.
  D. The second analyzes the claim made in the first.

39. Learning a second language helps students to gain certain essential academic skills.

In second-language acquisition, students develop logical thinking and improve their study skills.

What does the second sentence do?
  A. It repeats the same idea as stated in the first sentence.
  B. It sums up the points raised in the first sentence.
  C. It presents a solution to the problem mentioned in the first sentence.
  D. It expands on the claim made in the first sentence.

40. People in many countries around the world possess dual nationalism.

When a person acquires valid passports from more than one country, he or she becomes a dual national.

What does the second sentence do?
  A. It explains a concept mentioned in the first sentence.
  B. It restates the general idea given in the first sentence.
  C. It gives a solution to the problem described in the first sentence.
  D. It analyzes the evidence provided in the first sentence.

41. *Solve the seventeen following arithmetic problems and select the correct answer from the choices given. You may use paper to work out your answers.*

$3.75 + .004 + .179 = ?$
  A. 3.969
  B. 3.933
  C. .558
  D. 5.58

42. 6.55 × 1.2 = ?
    A. 7.68
    B. 7.86
    C. 78.6
    D. 786

43. Three people are going to contribute money for a new building. Person A will provide one-third of the money. Person B will contribute one-sixth of the money. What fraction represents Person C's contribution of money for the project?

    A. 2/3
    B. 5/6
    C. 1/2
    D. 16/18

44. Carmen uses one jar of coffee every 6 days. Approximately how many jars of coffee does she use per month?
    A. 2
    B. 3
    C. 5
    D. 6

45. Jonathan can run 3 miles in 25 minutes. If he maintains this pace, how long will it take him to run 12 miles?
    A. 1 hour and 15 minutes
    B. 1 hour and 40 minutes
    C. 1 hour and 45 minutes
    D. 3 hours

46. The price of T-shirts is $10 each and the price of jeans is $15 each. Jack went shopping for T-shirts and jeans, and he paid $70 in total. In this purchase, he bought 2 pairs of jeans. How many T-shirts did he buy?
    A. 3
    B. 4
    C. 6
    D. 10

47. A census shows that 1,008,942 people live in New Town, and 709,002 people live in Old Town. Which of the following numbers is the best estimate of how many more people live in New Town than in Old Town?
    A. 330,000
    B. 300,000
    C. 33,000
    D. 30,000

48. In a high school, 17 out of every 20 students participate in a sport. If there are 800 students at the high school, what is the total number of students that participate in a sport?
    A. 120
    B. 640
    C. 680
    D. 720

72

49. A baseball team had 32 games this season and lost 25 percent of them. How many games did the team lose?
   A. 8
   B. 16
   C. 18
   D. 24

50. A new skyscraper is being erected in the city center. The foundation of the building extends 1,135 feet below ground. The building itself, when erected, will measure 13,975 feet above ground. Which of the following is the best estimate of the distance between the deepest point of the foundation below ground and the top of the erected building above ground?
   A. 12,000 feet
   B. 13,000 feet
   C. 14,000 feet
   D. 15,000 feet

51. $5\frac{1}{2} - 2\frac{1}{4} = ?$
   A. $3\frac{1}{4}$
   B. $3\frac{1}{8}$
   C. $3\frac{1}{6}$
   D. $3\frac{2}{4}$

52. Mrs. Johnson is going to give candy to the students in her class. The first bag of candy that she has contains 43 pieces. The second contains 28 pieces, and the third contains 31 pieces. If there are 34 students in Mrs. Johnson's class, and the candy is divided equally among all of the students, how many pieces of candy will each student receive?
   A. 3 pieces
   B. 4 pieces
   C. 5 pieces
   D. 51 pieces

53. A classroom has enough desks to accommodate 85 students. Dr. Smith's class uses 68 of the available desks in this classroom. What percentage of the desks remain empty during Dr. Smith's class?
   A. 17%
   B. 20%
   C. 25%
   D. 80%

54. $2.25 + .555 + .001 = ?$
   A. 2.581
   B. 2.806
   C. 2.905
   D. 7.81

55. Mary bought a shirt on sale for $9. The original price of the shirt was $12. What was the percentage of the discount on the sale?
    A. 0.25%
    B. 25%
    C. 33%
    D. 50%

56. During each flight, a flight attendant must count the number of passengers on board the aircraft. The morning flight had 52 passengers more than the evening flight, and there were 540 passengers in total on the two flights that day. How many passengers were there on the evening flight?
    A. 244
    B. 296
    C. 488
    D. 540

57. $12 \div 80 = ?$
    A. .015
    B. .15
    C. 1.5
    D. 15

58. *Solve the twelve following algebra problems and select the correct answer from the choices given. You may use paper to work out your answers.*

    $(2x - 3y)^2 = ?$
    A. $4x^2 + 9y^2 - 12xy$
    B. $4x^2 + 9y^2 + 12xy$
    C. $4x^2 + 9y^2$
    D. $4x^2 - 9y^2$

59. If $3x - 2(x + 5) = -8$, then $x = ?$
    A. -12
    B. 12
    C. -2
    D. 2

60. $(x^2 - x - 6) \div (x - 3) = ?$
    A. $x + 2$
    B. $x - 2$
    C. $x^2 + x + 2$
    D. $x^2 + x - 2$

61. $(2 + -12) \div 5 = ?$
    A. 2
    B. $2^4/_5$
    C. -2
    D. $-2^4/_5$

62. If X represents the number of oranges purchased at 30 cents each and Y represents the number of lemons purchased at 35 cents each, which equation below represents the total value of the purchase?
    A. X + Y
    B. .65(X + Y)
    C. .35X + .30Y
    D. .30X + .35Y

63. If circle A has a radius of 0.5 and circle B has a radius of 0.3, what is the difference in area between the two circles?
    A. -0.65π
    B. 0.16π
    C. 1.6π
    D. 2.41π

64. What is the value of the expression $3x^2 + 4xy - y^2$ when $x = 2$ and $y = -2$?
    A. -8
    B. 0
    C. 8
    D. 24

65. $(3x - y)(2x + y) = ?$
    A. $x^2 + xy - y^2$
    B. $x^2 + xy + y^2$
    C. $6x^2 + xy - y^2$
    D. $6x^2 + xy + y^2$

66. $\sqrt{6} \times \sqrt{5} = ?$
    A. 11
    B. 30
    C. $\sqrt{11}$
    D. $\sqrt{30}$

67. $-2(7 - 3) - 5(3 - 4) = ?$
    A. -13
    B. -3
    C. 3
    D. 13

68. $25 - {}^2/_3 X > 21$, then $X < ?$
    A. $X < 7$
    B. $X < 6$
    C. $X < -7$
    D. $X < -6$

75

69. $8ab^2(3ab^4 + 2b) = ?$

    A. $11a^2b^6 + 10ab^3$

    B. $24a^2b^8 + 16ab^3$

    C. $48ab^6 + 32ab^2$

    D. $24a^2b^6 + 16ab^3$

70. Solve *the twenty following college-level math problems and select the correct answer from the choices given. You may use paper to work out your answers.*

If Ç is a special operation defined by $(x\ ç\ y) = (3x - 2y)$ and $(6\ ç\ z) = 8$, then $z = ?$

    A. 1
    B. 3
    C. 5
    D. 6

71. $\dfrac{5}{12x} + \dfrac{4}{10x^2} = ?$

    A. $\dfrac{9}{120x^3}$

    B. $\dfrac{48x}{50x^2}$

    C. $\dfrac{29}{12x}$

    D. $\dfrac{25x + 24}{60x^2}$

72. $(-5)^{-2} = ?$

    A. -25

    B. $-\dfrac{1}{25}$

    C. $\dfrac{1}{25}$

    D. 25

73. In the standard (x, y) plane, what is the distance between $(3\sqrt{3}, -1)$ and $(6\sqrt{3}, 2)$?

    A. 6
    B. 27
    C. 36
    D. $3\sqrt{3} + 1$

74. Perform the operation: $\sqrt{5}\,(\sqrt{20} - \sqrt{5})$

    A. $5\sqrt{15}$

    B. $\sqrt{45}$

    C.   25

    D.   5

75. $\dfrac{5 \times (7 - 4) + 3 \times 8}{2 \times (3 - 1)} = ?$

    A. $\dfrac{90}{4}$

    B. $\dfrac{39}{4}$

    C.   240

    D.   60

76. Solve by elimination:

    $x + 5y = 24$

    $8x + 2y = 40$

    A.   (4, 4)

    B.   (−4, 4)

    C.   (40, 4)

    D.   (4, 38)

77. Perform the operation: $(4x - 3)(5x^2 + 12x + 11) = ?$

    A. $20x^3 + 33x^2 + 80x - 33$

    B. $20x^3 + 33x^2 + 80x + 33$

    C. $20x^3 + 33x^2 + 8x - 33$

    D. $20x^3 + 33x^2 - 8x - 33$

78. $\sqrt{6x^3}\,\sqrt{24x^5} = ?$

    A. $12\sqrt{x^{15}}$

    B. $\sqrt{30x^8}$

    C. $12x^4$

    D. $144x^4$

79. $\sqrt{18} + 3\sqrt{32} + 5\sqrt{8} = ?$

    A. $17\sqrt{2}$

    B. $25\sqrt{2}$

    C. $8\sqrt{58}$

    D. $15\sqrt{58}$

80. Which equation represents the slope-intercept formula for the following data:

Through (4, 5); $m = {}^{-3}\!/\!_5$

    A. $y = -\dfrac{3}{5}x + 5$

    B. $y = -\dfrac{12}{5}x - 5$

    C. $y = -\dfrac{3}{5}x - \dfrac{37}{5}$

    D. $y = -\dfrac{3}{5}x + \dfrac{37}{5}$

81. The perimeter of a rectangle is 48 meters. If the width were doubled and the length were increased by 5 meters, the perimeter would be 92 meters. What are the length and width of the rectangle?

    A. width = 17, length = 7

    B. width = 7, length = 17

    C. width = 34, length = 14

    D. width = 24, length = 46

82. For all $a \neq b$,

$$\dfrac{\dfrac{5a}{b}}{\dfrac{2a}{a-b}} = ?$$

    A. $\dfrac{10a^2}{ab - b^2}$ B. $\dfrac{a-b}{2b}$ C. $\dfrac{5a-5}{2}$ D. $\dfrac{5a-5b}{2b}$

83. Perform the operation and express as one fraction: $\dfrac{1}{a+1}+\dfrac{1}{a}$

    A. $\dfrac{2}{2a+1}$

    B. $\dfrac{a+1}{a}$

    C. $\dfrac{a^2+a}{2a+1}$

    D. $\dfrac{2a+1}{a^2+a}$

84. $\sqrt[3]{\dfrac{8}{27}}$ = ?

    A. $\dfrac{2}{3}$

    B. $\dfrac{4}{9}$

    C. $\dfrac{2}{9}$

    D. $\dfrac{\sqrt{8}}{9}$

85. $\dfrac{\sqrt{48}}{3}+\dfrac{5\sqrt{5}}{6}$ = ?

    A. $\dfrac{4\sqrt{3}+5\sqrt{5}}{6}$

    B. $\dfrac{8\sqrt{3}+5\sqrt{5}}{6}$

    C. $\dfrac{\sqrt{48}+5\sqrt{5}}{9}$

    D. $\dfrac{6\sqrt{48}+5\sqrt{5}}{18}$

86. Consider the vertex of an angle at the center of a circle. The diameter of the circle is 2. If the angle measures 45 degrees, what is the arc length relating to the angle?
    A. $\pi/4$
    B. $\pi/3$
    C. $\pi/2$
    D. π

87. Consider points A and B on a circle. The chord length of AB is equal to which of the following?
    A. The length of the arc connecting A and B.
    B. The length of the straight line connecting A and B.
    C. The measurement of the angle adjacent to A and B.
    D. $(A + B)/\pi$

88. The tangent of x is equivalent to which of the following?
    A. $\sin x + \cos x$
    B. $\sin x \div \cos x$
    C. $\sin x - \cos x$
    D. $1 \div (\sin x + \cos x)$

89. The equation $4 = \log_3 81$ is equivalent to which of the following?
    A. $243 \div 4$
    B. $3 = \log_4 81$
    C. $4^3 = 81$
    D. $3^4 = 81$

ACCUPLACER PRACTICE TEST 3 – ANSWERS

1. The correct answer is D. The phrase *while at the mall* modifies the pronoun "I." So "I" needs to come after this phrase.

2. The correct answer is C. When a compound sentence contains the word "just" to describe an action that has recently been completed, the past perfect tense [had + past participle] should be used in the part of the sentence containing the word "just."

3. The correct answer is D. This question is about the use of punctuation. "Then our plans changed" is an independent clause. It has a grammatical subject [our plans] and a verb [changed]. According to traditional rules of grammar, "and" is a coordinating conjunction, used to combine phrases or clauses within a sentence. Since "and" is a conjunction, we should avoid beginning sentences with "and." So the word "and" should be included within a single sentence and preceded by a comma.

4. The correct answer is C. This question is about gerunds, also known as -ing words or verbal nouns. Note that the -ing form is usually used when discussing activities or hobbies.

5. The correct answer is A. Exasperated is a past participle phrase that describes Bill. So the sentence is correct as it is written.

6. The correct answer is A. The words "that would accommodate all of his oversized furniture" form a dependent relative clause. A dependent relative clause containing "that" is not preceded by a comma.

7. The correct answer is C. Punctuation should be enclosed within the final quotation mark when giving dialogue. The word *exclaimed* shows that the exclamation point is needed.

8. The correct answer is B. The phrase "in spite of" must be followed by a noun or noun phrase. "In spite of" should not be followed by a clause. The -ing form "studying" is used as a gerund (a verbal noun) in this sentence.

9. The correct answer is D. This question tests your knowledge of the comparative and superlative forms. Use the comparative form (-er) when comparing *two* things. If you are comparing *more than two* things, you must use the superlative form (-est).

10. The correct answer is C. This question tests your knowledge of conditional sentence structures. Conditional sentences often begin with the word *if*. Conditional sentences may address hypothetical or imaginary situations. This sentence mentions a hypothetical situation. Therefore, the simple present tense (steal) is used in the "If" clause, and the modal verb (could) is used in the main part of the sentence. The two parts of conditional sentences beginning with "if" must be separated by a comma.

11. The correct answer is B. The new sentence is: Once they had checked the extent of the man's injuries, the paramedics put him into the ambulance. Clauses that begin with "once" need to contain the past perfect tense. The past perfect tense is formed with "had" plus the past participle, which is "checked" in this sentence.

12. The correct answer is A. The new sentence is: I was embarrassed when the professor praised my exam score in front of the other students. The word "when" forms a subordinate clause in the second part of the new sentence. Since the first part of the new sentence contains the past tense (was), the second part of the new sentence also contains the past tense (praised). The words "the professor" form the grammatical subject of the subordinate clause. Therefore, the pronoun "he" is not needed.

13. The correct answer is A. The new sentence is: Like Minnesota, Wisconsin gets extremely cold in the winter. The phrase "like Minnesota" is an adjectival phrase that modifies the noun "Wisconsin." Therefore, "Wisconsin" must come directly after the comma.

14. The correct answer is C. The new sentence is: The Grand Canyon is a popular tourist destination because it is rich in natural beauty and abundant in wildlife. The word "because" is used to join a subordinate clause to a sentence. Remember that clauses are distinct from phrases because clauses contain both a grammatical subject and a verb. "It" is the grammatical subject in the subordinate clause of the new sentence and "is" is the verb.

15. The correct answer is D. The new sentence is: My sister, who was ill with the flu, stayed home from school. The comma after "my sister" indicates that a relative clause must be used. Remember that relative clauses can include the following words: who, which, that, whom, whose.

16. The correct answer is C. The new sentence is: In the event of rain tomorrow, the picnic will have to be canceled. The phrase "in the event of" should be followed by a noun or noun phrase. In addition, the verb must be changed to the passive from, using the verb "be."

17. The correct answer is B. The new sentence would be constructed as follows: The team was so disappointed when it lost the championship game. The grammatical construction is similar to question 12 above.

18. The correct answer is A. The new sentence would be constructed as follows: Although he trained for years, he was not selected for the Olympics. Sentences that begin with "although" introduce an unexpected result to a situation.

19. The correct answer is C. The new sentence is: Watching television, he fell asleep and began snoring. Phrases that begin with verbs in the -ing form are known as present participle phrases. In the new sentence, the present participle phrase "watching television" modifies "he." Therefore, "he" must come directly after the comma.

20. The correct answer is D. The new sentence is as follows: Suffering from homesickness is common among international students who study in the United States. In the new sentence, the -ing form (suffering) is used as a gerund. So "suffering from homesickness" is the grammatical subject of the new sentence. The grammatical subject is followed by a verb (is) and an adjective (common). Note that "commonality" is a noun.

21. The correct answer is C. We know that the passage is going to give historical information because the topic sentence [defined as the first sentence of a paragraph] contains the phrase "was founded in 1876." Answers A and B give *specific* points that are mentioned in the passage, not the main idea. Answer D is incorrect because no criticisms are stated in the passage.

22. The correct answer is A. The passage states that "computer-to-computer trading could result in a downturn in the stock market." Further, this downturn could result in a "computer-led stock market crash." In order to avoid these negative results, the regulations are needed. Answers B and C are not stated in the passage. Answer D is incorrect because the passage talks about how the use of computers has *changed* over time.

23. The correct answer is C. The last sentence of the passage explains the purpose of or reasons for the aircraft crash investigations. Answers A and B are too specific. Answer D is not stated in the passage.

24. The correct answer is C. The last sentence of the passage states: "It took an expedition of Italian scientists, who used a surfeit of technological devices, to disprove Wallerstein's claim." In other words, the Italians proved that Everest was in fact higher than K-2. [Note: *Surfeit* means a large or abundant amount of something.]

25. The correct answer is A. The words "sinister undertones" and "arguably" in the passage demonstrate that cloning is a controversial subject. Answer C is not implied in the passage. There is information in the passage to suggest that answers B and D are incorrect.

26. The correct answer is D. The passage uses the words "myths," "misconceptions," and "mistakenly" to show that most people do not have the correct knowledge about tornadoes.

27. The correct answer is B. When explaining the idea of assimilation, the passage uses the phrase "are examples of" to show that breast and bottle feeding are being used as examples. Note that "exemplify" means to give an example.

28. The correct answer is A. The passage concludes by stating: "there was a surge in artifacts excavated from African and Asian localities by the late 1900s." "Surge" means to increase suddenly from a small or low amount. If these findings suddenly increased at the end of the century, one could assume that they were limited at the beginning of the century. Answers B and D are incorrect according to the passage. Answer C is an overgeneralization.

29. The correct answer is A. The topic sentence contains the word "originated." Only one century is mentioned in the passage, so answer B is incorrect. Answer C is too specific. Answer D is not stated in the passage.

30. The correct answer is B. The passage states: "Food additives are detrimental to the health for a number of reasons." This statement is followed by two reasons: the link to disease and the blockage of nutrients.

31. The correct answer is D. If there are problems traveling abroad, one would expect that most people would not want to do it. However, in spite of the problems caused by miscommunication, more and more tourists travel overseas. Therefore, the unexpected result in the second sentence creates a contrast with the statement made in the first sentence.

32. The correct answer is A. People are now without homes because the hurricane destroyed their homes. So the homelessness is the effect or the result of the hurricane.

33. The correct answer is B. The isolation mentioned in the second sentence opposes the idea of "getting along" (or cooperation) mentioned in the first sentence. Therefore, the sentences contradict each other.

34. The correct answer is C. The first sentence mentions the problems associated with pollution, namely its negative effects on the environment. The second sentence talks about regulations which attempt to reduce the pollution, thereby solving the problem.

35. The correct answer is D. We would expect people to fulfill their duties and responsibilities. Although voting is an important duty, a large percentage of people do not vote. Therefore, it is an unexpected outcome.

36. The correct answer is A. The phrase "so-called broken homes" in the second sentence is a now outdated expression that refers to children whose parents are divorced. Both sentences talk about the negative effects of divorce on children and their academic achievement.

37. The correct answer is C. The first sentence talks generally about the hardships caused by colonization. The second sentence mentions the deaths caused by new diseases as a specific example of one type of distress or hardship. In other words, the second sentence is much more specific than the first.

38. The correct answer is B. Despite the penalties for cheating, some students still prefer to buy their essays, which is of course a form of cheating. Therefore, the second sentence mentions an unexpected result in order to provide a contrast.

39. The correct answer is D. The first sentence makes a limited claim by using the word *certain*. The second sentence expands on the first one because logical thinking and study skills are two essential academic skills. The second sentence is much more specific than the first one, so we cannot say that they repeat the same idea.

40. The correct answer is A. The second sentence deals only with dual nationalism, which is one specific aspect of the first sentence. The conditions for dual nationalism are defined or explained in the second sentence. Therefore, we cannot say that the sentences restate the same idea.

41. The correct answer is B. Be sure to line all of the decimals up in a column like this:

3.750
0.004
0.179
3.993

42. The correct answer is B. Be sure to put the decimal point in the correct position after you do the long multiplication. If we remove the decimal points:

655 x 12 = 6550 + 1330 = 7860

6.55 has a decimal two places from the right. 1.2 has a decimal point 1 place from the right. So we know that we have to put the decimal point *three* numbers from the right on the final product of 7860. Therefore the final answer is 7.860, which is simplified to 7.86

43. The correct answer is C. The sum of contributions from all three people must be equal to 100%, simplified to 1. In other words, they make up the whole contribution by paying in together:

A + B + C = 1

1/3 + 1/6 + C = 1

Now, find the lowest common denominator of the fractions:

2/6 + 1/6 + C = 1

Therefore, C = 3/6, which is simplified to 1/2.

44. The correct answer is C. This is an estimation type question expressed as a practical problem. Every month has 28 to 31 days, so we can estimate this as 30 days for the average month. Then divide 30 by 6 to determine the answer:

average days in a month ÷ days of usage = number of items
30 ÷ 6 = 5

45. The correct answer is B. Jonathan runs 3 miles in 25 minutes, so in order to determine how long he need to runs 12 miles, we multiply 25 by 4. In other words, since he runs 3 miles in 25 minutes, he will need four times as long to run 12 miles (since 3 times 4 equals 12).

25 minutes × 4 = 100 minutes

100 minutes = 1 hour and 40 minutes

46. The correct answer is B. If each item has a different price, you must assign a different variable to each item. So, let's say that the number of jeans is *J* and the number of T-shirts is *T*. Now let's make an equation to express the above problem:

(*T* × $10) + (*J* × $15) = $70

We know that the number of jeans is 2, so let's put that in the equation and solve it:

$(T \times \$10) + (J \times \$15) = \$70$
$(T \times \$10) + (2 \times \$15) = \$70$
$(T \times \$10) + 30 = \$70$
$(T \times \$10) + 30 - 30 = \$70 - \$30$
$(T \times \$10) = \$40$
$\$10T = \$40$
$\$10T \div \$10 = \$40 \div \$10$
$T = 4$

47. The correct answer is B. Round the 1,008,942 people living in New Town up to 1,010,000 and round the 709,002 people living in Old Town up to 710,000. Then subtract: 1,010,000 − 710,000 = 300,000

48. The correct answer is C. Divide 800 by 20 to get 40; in other words, there are 40 groups consisting of 20 students each in the school. Then multiply 40 by 17 to determine how many students in total participate in a sport: 40 × 17 = 680

49. The correct answer is A. For this problem, you must do long multiplication:

```
    32
×  .25
  1.60
  6.40
  8.00
```

50. The correct answer is D. For practical estimation problems like this, round the numbers up or down to the nearest thousand. 13,975 is rounded up to 14,000 and 1,135 is rounded down to 1,000. Then add to get the total distance from top to bottom: 14,000 + 1,000 = 15,000

51. The correct answer is A. If the fraction on the first mixed number is greater than the fraction on the second mixed number, you can subtract the whole numbers and the fractions separately. Remember to use the lowest common denominator on the fractions:

5 − 2 = 3

1/2 − 1/4 = 2/4 − 1/4 = 1/4

Therefore, the result is 3¼.

52. The correct answer is A. First determine the total amount of candy: 43 + 28 + 31 = 102 pieces. Then divide the total amount of candy by the total number of students to determine how many pieces each student will receive. 102 total pieces ÷ 34 total students = 3 pieces per student

53. The correct answer is B. We know that the class uses 68 of the desks. However, the question is asking you about the *empty* desks. So first determine how many desks are empty: 85 − 68 = 17

Now divide the number of empty desks into the number of total desks to get the percentage:

17 ÷ 85 = .20
.20 = 20%

54. The correct answer is B.

2.250
0.555
<u>0.001</u>
2.806

55. The correct answer is B. In order to calculate a discount, you must first determine how much the item was marked down: $12 – $9 = $3

Then divide the mark down by the original price: 3 ÷ 12 = 0.25

Finally, convert the decimal to a percentage: 0.25 = 25%

56. The correct answer is A. Take the total for both flights and subtract the amount of passengers that the morning flight had in excess of those on the evening flight: 540 – 52 = 488

Now divide by 2 to determine how many passengers are on the evening flight: 488 ÷ 2 = 244

57. The correct answer is B.

$$
\begin{array}{r}
.15 \\
80\overline{)12.00} \\
\underline{8.0} \\
4.00 \\
\underline{4.00} \\
0
\end{array}
$$

58. The correct answer is A. Use the F-O-I-L method. Multiply the terms two at a time from each of the two parts of the equation in this order: First - Outside - Inside - Last

$(2x – 3y)^2 = (2x – 3y)(2x – 3y)$

FIRST: $2x \times 2x = 4x^2$
OUTSIDE: $2x \times –3y = –6xy$
INSIDE: $–3y \times 2x = –6xy$
LAST: $–3y \times –3y = 9y^2$

Then we add all of the above parts together to get: $4x^2 + 9y^2 – 12xy$

59. The correct answer is D. Perform multiplication on the items in parentheses first:

$3x – 2(x + 5) = –8$
$3x – 2x – 10 = –8$

Then deal with the integers by putting them on one side of the equation as follows:

$3x – 2x – 10 + 10 = –8 + 10$
$3x – 2x = 2$

Then solve for x:

$3x - 2x = 2$
$1x = 2$
$x = 2$

60. The correct answer is A. Do long division of the polynomial.

$$
\begin{array}{r}
x + 2 \\
x - 3 \overline{)\,x^2 - x - 6} \\
\underline{x^2 - 3x} \\
2x - 6 \\
\underline{2x - 6} \\
0
\end{array}
$$

61. The correct answer is C. Deal with the part of the equation inside the parentheses first:

$(2 + -12) \div 5 = -10 \div 5$

Then do the division: $-10 \div 5 = -2$

62. The correct answer is D. Each item needs to have its own variable: X for oranges and Y for lemons.

The total value of the oranges is .30X
The total value of the lemons is .35Y

The total value of the purchase is the sum of the values of these two variables: .30X + .35Y

63. The correct answer is B. The area of a circle is always: π times the radius squared.

Therefore, the area of circle A is: $0.5^2\pi = 0.25\pi$

The area of circle B is: $0.3^2\pi = 0.09\pi$

To calculate the difference in area between the two circles, we then subtract:

$0.25\pi - 0.09\pi = 0.16\pi$

64. The correct answer is A. To solve this problem, put in the values for x and y and multiply. Remember to be careful when multiplying negative numbers:

$3x^2 + 4xy - y^2 =$
$(3 \times 2^2) + (4 \times 2 \times -2) - (-2^2) =$
$(3 \times 2 \times 2) + (4 \times 2 \times -2) - (-2 \times -2) =$
$(3 \times 4) + (4 \times -4) - (4) =$
$12 + (-16) - 4 =$
$12 - 16 - 4 =$
-8

65. The correct answer is C. Use F-O-I-L:

FIRST: $3x \times 2x = 6x^2$
OUTSIDE: $3x \times y = 3xy$
INSIDE: $-y \times 2x = -2xy$
LAST: $-y \times y = -y^2$

Then add all of the above once you have completed F-O-I-L:

$6x^2 + 3xy + -2xy + -y^2 =$
$6x^2 + 3xy - 2xy - y^2 =$
$6x^2 + xy - y^2$

66. The correct answer is D. Multiply the numbers inside the square root symbols: $6 \times 5 = 30$

Then put this result inside a square root symbol for your answer: $\sqrt{30}$

67. The correct answer is B. Do the operations inside the parentheses first and be careful when multiplying the negative numbers.

$-2(7 - 3) - 5(3 - 4) =$
$-2(4) - 5(-1) =$
$(-2 \times 4) - (5 \times -1) =$
$-8 - (-5) =$
$-8 + 5 = -3$

68. The correct answer is B. Deal with the whole numbers on each side of the equation first:

$25 - {}^2/_3X > 21 =$
$(25 - 25) - {}^2/_3X > (21 - 25) =$
$-{}^2/_3X > -4$

Then with the fraction:

$-{}^2/_3X > -4 =$
$3 \times -{}^2/_3X > -4 \times 3 =$
$-2X > -12$

Then the remaining whole numbers:

$-2X > -12 =$
$-2X \div 2 > -12 \div 2 =$
$-X > -6$

Then, deal with the negative number:

$-X > -6 =$
$-X + 6 > -6 + 6 =$
$-X + 6 > 0$

Finally, isolate the unknown variable as a positive number:

$-X + 6 > 0 =$
$-X + X + 6 > 0 + X =$
$6 > X =$
$X < 6$

69. The correct answer is D. Remember to multiply the integers, but to add the exponents. Also remember that any variable times itself is equal to that variable squared. For example, $a \times a = a^2$

$$8ab^2(3ab^4 + 2b) =$$
$$(8ab^2 \times 3ab^4) + (8ab^2 \times 2b) =$$
$$24a^2b^6 + 16ab^3$$

70. The correct answer is C. We have the special operation defined as: $(x \,Ç\, y) = (3x - 2y)$. First of all, look at the relationship between the left-hand side and the right-hand side of this equation in order to determine which operations you need to perform on any new equation containing the operation Ç and variables x and y.

In other words, in any new equation:

Operation Ç is subtraction.
The number or variable immediately after the opening parenthesis will be multiplied by 3.
The number or variable immediately before the closing parenthesis will be multiplied by 2.

So, the new equation $(6 \,Ç\, z) = 8$ becomes $(6 \times 3 - 2 \times z) = 8$

Now solve for $(6 \times 3 - 2 \times z) = 8$

$(6 \times 3 - 2 \times z) = 8$
$18 - 2z = 8$
$18 - 18 - 2z = 8 - 18$
$-2z = -10$
$-2z \div -2 = -10 \div -2$
$z = 5$

71. The correct answer is D. First you have to find the lowest common denominator. Deal with the integers in the denominator, then with the variable. Ask yourself: What is the smallest possible number that is divisible by both 12 and by 10? The answer is 60. Alternatively, find the factors of 12 and 10, then multiply by the factor that they do not have in common. $12 = 2 \times 6$ and $10 = 2 \times 5$, so multiply 12 by 5 and 10 by 6 to arrive at 60 for the integer part of the denominator. Then deal with the variable. $x = x \times 1$ and $x^2 = x \times x$, so multiply $x^2 \times 1$ and $x \times x$, to get x^2 for the variable part of the denominator. In other words, the LCD is $60x^2$. Don't forget to multiply the numerator and denominator of each fraction by the same amounts:

$$\frac{5}{12x} + \frac{4}{10x^2} =$$

$$\frac{5x}{5x} \times \frac{5}{12x} + \frac{4}{10x^2} \times \frac{6}{6} =$$

$$\frac{25x}{60x^2} + \frac{24}{60x^2} =$$

$$\frac{25x + 24}{60x^2}$$

72. The correct answer is C. To answer this type of question, remember that $x^{-b} = \dfrac{1}{x^b}$

Therefore, $-5^{-2} = \dfrac{1}{-5^2} = \dfrac{1}{25}$

73. The correct answer is A. To solve problems asking for the distance between two points (x_1, y_1) and (x_2, y_2), you need to use the distance formula:

$$d = \sqrt{(x_2 - x_1)^2 + (y_2 - y_1)^2}$$

Now we need to put in the values stated: $(3\sqrt{3}, -1)$ and $(6\sqrt{3}, 2)$

$$d = \sqrt{(6\sqrt{3} - 3\sqrt{3})^2 + (2 - -1)^2}$$
$$d = \sqrt{(3\sqrt{3})^2 + (3)^2}$$
$$d = \sqrt{(9 \times 3) + 9}$$
$$d = \sqrt{27 + 9}$$
$$d = \sqrt{36}$$
$$d = 6$$

74. The correct answer is D. Multiply the number in front of the parentheses by each number inside the parentheses. Then find the square roots and subtract.

$$\sqrt{5}(\sqrt{20} - \sqrt{5}) =$$
$$(\sqrt{5} \times \sqrt{20}) - (\sqrt{5} \times \sqrt{5}) =$$
$$\sqrt{100} - \sqrt{25} =$$
$$10 - 5 = 5$$

75. The correct answer is B. For this type of problem, do the operations inside the parentheses first, then do multiplication and division, then the addition and subtraction.

$$\frac{5 \times (7-4) + 3 \times 8}{2 \times (3-1)} =$$

$$\frac{5 \times 3 + 3 \times 8}{2 \times 2} =$$

$$\frac{15 + 24}{4} = \frac{39}{4}$$

76. The correct answer is A. Here we have two equations:

$$x + 5y = 24$$
$$8x + 2y = 40$$

In order to solve by elimination, you need to subtract the second equation from the first equation. So look at the *x* variable of the second equation. Here we have 8*x*. So in order to eliminate the *x* variable, we need to multiply the first equation by 8 and then subtract the second equation.

$$x + 5y = 24$$
$$(8 \times x) + (5y \times 8) = (24 \times 8)$$
$$8x + 40y = 192$$

Now subtract the two equations:

$$\begin{array}{r} 8x + 40y = 192 \\ -(8x + 2y = 40) \\ \hline 38y = 152 \end{array}$$

Then solve for y:

$$38y = 152$$
$$38y \div 38 = 152 \div 38$$
$$y = 4$$

Now put in the values for *y* and solve for *x*:

$$x + 5y = 24$$
$$x + (5 \times 4) = 24$$
$$x + 20 = 24$$
$$x + 20 - 20 = 24 - 20$$
$$x = 4$$

77. The correct answer is C. For problems like this one, you need to multiply the first term in the first set of parentheses by all of the terms in the second set of parentheses. Then multiply the second term in the first set of parentheses by all of the terms in the second set of parentheses. Then simplify, remembering to be careful about the negative signs on the second set of parentheses.

$$(4x-3)(5x^2+12x+11)=$$
$$((5x^2\times 4x)+(12x\times 4x)+(11\times 4x))-((5x^2\times 3)+(12x\times 3)+(11\times 3))=$$
$$(20x^3+48x^2+44x)-(15x^2+36x+33)=$$
$$(20x^3+48x^2+44x)-15x^2-36x-33=$$
$$20x^3+48x^2-15x^2+44x-36x-33=$$
$$20x^3+33x^2+8x-33$$

78. The correct answer is C. Multiply the integers inside the two square root signs and add the exponents when multiplying the variables. Then find the square root, if possible.

$$\sqrt{6x^3}\sqrt{24x^5}=$$
$$\sqrt{144x^8}=$$
$$\sqrt{(12\times 12)(x^4\times x^4)}=$$
$$12x^4$$

79. The correct answer is B. Factor the integers inside each of the square root signs and then do the addition.

$$\sqrt{18}+3\sqrt{32}+5\sqrt{8}=$$
$$\sqrt{2\times 9}+3\sqrt{2\times 16}+5\sqrt{2\times 4}=$$
$$\sqrt{2\times(3\times 3)}+3\sqrt{2\times(4\times 4)}+5\sqrt{2\times(2\times 2)}=$$
$$3\sqrt{2}+(3\times 4)\sqrt{2}+(5\times 2)\sqrt{2}=$$
$$3\sqrt{2}+12\sqrt{2}+10\sqrt{2}=$$
$$25\sqrt{2}$$

80. The correct answer is D. You will remember that the slope intercept formula is: $y = mx + b$, where m is the slope and b is the y intercept. You will also remember the slope formula: $m = \dfrac{y_2-y_1}{x_2-x_1}$

We are given the slope, as well as the point (4,5), so first we need to put those values into the slope formula.

$$\frac{y_2-y_1}{x_2-x_1}=-\frac{3}{5}$$
$$\frac{5-y_1}{4-x_1}=-\frac{3}{5}$$
$$\left(4-x_1\right)\frac{5-y_1}{4-x_1}=-\frac{3}{5}\left(4-x_1\right)$$

$$5 - y_1 = -\frac{3}{5}(4 - x_1)$$

Now put in 0 for x_1 in the slope formula in order to find b (the y intercept is the point at which the line crosses the y axis).

$$5 - y_1 = -\frac{3}{5}(4 - x_1)$$

$$5 - y_1 = -\frac{3}{5}(4 - 0)$$

$$5 - y_1 = -\frac{3 \times 4}{5}$$

$$5 - y_1 = -\frac{12}{5}$$

$$5 - 5 - y_1 = -\frac{12}{5} - 5$$

$$-y_1 = -\frac{12}{5} - 5$$

$$-y_1 \times -1 = \left(-\frac{12}{5} - 5\right) \times -1$$

$$y_1 = \frac{12}{5} + 5$$

$$y_1 = \frac{12}{5} + (5 \times \frac{5}{5})$$

$$y_1 = \frac{12 + 25}{5}$$

$$y_1 = \frac{37}{5}$$

Now put this value into the slope intercept formula:

$y = mx + b$

$$y = -\frac{3}{5}x + \frac{37}{5}$$

81. The correct answer is A. The perimeter of a rectangle is equal to 2 times the length (L) plus two times the width (W). We can express this concept as an equation: P = 2L + 2W.

Now set up formulas for the perimeters both before and after the increase.

STEP 1 – Before the increase:

P = 2L + 2W
48 = 2L + 2W
48 ÷ 2 = (2L + 2W) ÷ 2
24 = L + W
24 – W = L + W – W
24 – W = L

STEP 2 – After the increase (length is increased by 5 and width is doubled):

P = 2L + 2W
92 = 2(L + 5) + (2×2)W
92 = 2L + 10 + 4W
92 –10 = 2L + 10 – 10 + 4W
82 = 2L + 4W

Then solve by substitution. In this case, we substitute 24 – W (which we calculated in the "before" equation in step 1) for L in the "after" equation calculated in step 2, in order to solve for W:

82 = 2L + 4W
82 = 2(24 – W) + 4W
82 = 48 – 2W + 4W
82 – 48 = 48 – 48 – 2W + 4W
82 – 48 = – 2W + 4W
34 = –2W + 4W
34 = 2W
34 ÷ 2 = 2W ÷ 2
17 = W

Then substitute the value for W in order to solve for L.

24 – W = L
24 – 17 = L
7 = L

82. The correct answer is D. When you have fractions in the numerator and denominator of another fraction, you can divide the two fractions as follows:

$$\frac{\dfrac{5a}{b}}{\dfrac{2a}{a-b}} =$$

$$\frac{5a}{b} \div \frac{2a}{a-b}$$

Then invert and multiply just like you would for any other fraction.

$$\frac{5a}{b} \div \frac{2a}{a-b} =$$

$$\frac{5a}{b} \times \frac{a-b}{2a} =$$

$$\frac{5a^2 - 5ab}{2ab}$$

Then simplify, if possible:

$$\frac{5a^2 - 5ab}{2ab} =$$

$$\frac{a(5a - 5b)}{a(2b)} =$$

$$\frac{5a - 5b}{2b}$$

83. The correct answer is D. Find the lowest common denominator and then simplify, if possible.

$$\frac{1}{a+1} + \frac{1}{a} = \frac{1}{a+1} \times \frac{a}{a} + \frac{1}{a} \times \frac{a+1}{a+1} =$$

$$\frac{a}{a^2 + a} + \frac{a+1}{a^2 + a} =$$

$$\frac{a + a + 1}{a^2 + a} = \frac{2a + 1}{a^2 + a}$$

84. The correct answer is A. Find the cube roots of the integers, factor, and then express as a rational number.

$$\sqrt[3]{\frac{8}{27}} = \sqrt[3]{\frac{2 \times 2 \times 2}{3 \times 3 \times 3}} = \frac{2}{3}$$

85. The correct answer is B. Find the lowest common denominator and then simplify, if possible.

$$\frac{\sqrt{48}}{3} + \frac{5\sqrt{5}}{6} =$$

$$\frac{\sqrt{48}}{3} \times \frac{2}{2} + \frac{5\sqrt{5}}{6} =$$

$$\frac{2\sqrt{48}}{6} + \frac{5\sqrt{5}}{6} =$$

$$\frac{2\sqrt{16 \times 3} + 5\sqrt{5}}{6} =$$

$$\frac{(2 \times 4)\sqrt{3} + 5\sqrt{5}}{6} =$$

$$\frac{8\sqrt{3} + 5\sqrt{5}}{6}$$

86. The correct answer is A. To solve this type of problem, you need these three principles:

Arc length is the distance on the outside (or circumference) of a circle.
The circumference of a circle is always π times the diameter.
There are 360 degrees in a circle.

The angle in this problem is 45 degrees.

$360 \div 45 = 8$; In other words, we are dealing with the circumference of 1/8 of the circle.

Given that the circumference of this circle is 2π, and we are dealing only with 1/8 of the circle, then the arc length for this angle is:

$2\pi \div 8 = \pi/4$

87. The correct answer is B. A chord is a straight line between two points on a circle.

88. The correct answer is B. The tangent is always equal to the sin $\div$ cos.

89. The correct answer is D. $A = \log_b C$ is always equal to $b^A = C$

18061899R00053

Made in the USA
Lexington, KY
12 October 2012